Contents

Preface

*I treasure this strange combination
found in very few persons: a fierce
desire for life as well as a lucid
perception of the ultimate futility
of the quest.*
Madeleine Gobeil

How to Manage a Nonprofit Organization represents, to the author's knowledge, the first attempt to provide the broadest possible range of information relating to the day-to-day effectiveness of nonprofit community organizations. Although it would be unwise to claim that this manual contains all you need to know on the subject, it does incorporate much new and old information and structures it to emphasize how all parts of an organization must interrelate in order to achieve effective action. Nonprofits, because of their limited resources, too often have a tendency to put all their eggs in one organizational basket, such as fund raising or management. To counter this, *How to Manage a Nonprofit Organization* stresses the seven basic areas of operation essential to most nonprofit organizations and urges that work groups be formed to support these functions and to ensure that they work cooperatively alongside each other.

I have written the manual with the assumption that 75 percent of the organizational problems facing nonprofits are shared by all groups, even though they may operate in the different fields of fitness, education, welfare, or arts and culture. This assumption holds true whether the group is large or small, rural or urban, service or issue oriented. *How to Manage a Nonprofit Organization* should be of interest to individuals who sit on a board of directors or are professionally employed by a nonprofit organization, and to those who serve as volunteers at all organizational levels. In addition, persons who work for governments, foundations and corporations and any others who provide support for community groups should be able to use this manual to assist them in their work.

How to Manage a Nonprofit Organization can be read from cover to cover; in fact, I would encourage the reader to do just that. However, it is also a reference work and has been designed to be consulted selectively on specific topics. To get the most out of the manual, it is important to pursue the references listed at the end of most sections. To make the manual work for you, work for it. Be creative; adopt and adapt its suggestions—it's meant to encourage you to explore new ideas.

It is merely a beginning!

People to thank

This manual is a result of work I have been involved with over the past ten years. There are literally hundreds of people to thank for their kindness and support. Of particular note are Dr. John Frei, who taught me the value of believing in the effort of others; Professor Anthony Adamson, for his humour and optimism tempered with a gorgeous irreverence for things sacred; Dr. Reva Gerstein, who toward finding new solutions taught me the value of questioning the accepted; Sylvia and Ray, my dear friends at Open Circle Theatre, who so patiently endured those periods AWOL that allowed this manual to be.

I am deeply indebted to my researcher Christine Vicary, for her care and industry and to Joanne Cooper, my consulting partner, who, like a squirrel, stockpiled for years much of the literature to support the manual's text and then, characteristically, in the face of impossible obstacles, turned publisher. Without her, what you have in your hands would probably not exist. I am grateful to Phyllis Stevens, who typed finger-raw into the night; Diane Dewey, for her moral support and dippy quotes; Gussy, a dog, in spite of; and finally, all those people scattered about Toronto, an amazing team linked by taxi cabs and courier services, who edited, designed, typeset and printed.

A note on terminology

An attempt has been made to keep terminology simple and consistent. However, it is worth noting that "organization," "community group," "nonprofit group," for the manual's purposes mean the same thing. Also "board of directors" and "policy-setting group" are interchangeable terms.

Finally, a special note for women readers. The pronouns he and him are used for editorial efficiency and ease of reading. I join many other writers in hoping that someone will soon invent words that will serve both sexes equally and save those who believe in the rights of women from experiencing mild traumas.

John Fisher

Beginnings

You see things and you say "Why?" But I dream things that never were; and I say "Why not?"

George Bernard Shaw

1

Keeping your dream alive

Practical people would be more practical if they would take a little more time for dreaming.

J.P. McEvoy

The fact that you are reading this manual shows you have a dream — an ideal to be realized. Doubtless you are aware that many difficulties will emerge before your dream becomes a reality. Grim determination provides less fuel than a positive attitude. Here are some suggestions:

1. Work hard, but rest when you are tired — don't become a liability.
2. Be open to other people — they may enrich your dream.
3. Be realistic.
4. Be patient.
5. Trust others, but don't be naive.
6. Be organized. Do what you say you will do.
7. Persevere — there always is more than one way of doing anything.
8. Take time away from the front line at least once a week to regain objectivity.
9. Be decisive, but never rush an important decision.
10. Don't be scared (or abusive) of others, particularly those with the trappings of power and success — it's all in *your* mind.
11. Be prepared for frustration and lonely times.
12. Keep a clear picture of what you want to see done.
13. See problems as challenges. Don't let day-to-day difficulties get to you.
14. Above all, retain your dream in one piece at all times. Don't give up on it until it's *proved* unworkable. You could be ahead of your time.

*We must believe that it is the darkest before
the dawn of a beautiful new world. We will
see it when we believe it.*
Saul Alinsky

Good Reading

H. B. Gelatt. *Deciding*. College Board Publications, Box 2815, Princeton, New Jersey 08540. $2.50. (*Deciding: A Leader's Guide* is free with each ten copies ordered.) A guide to making decisions.

*Advice from an old carpenter:
measure twice, saw once.*
Unknown

Brainstorming

*I'm always looking for a new idea
that will be more productive than
its cost.*
David Rockefeller

This is an all-purpose technique for getting ten to ten thousand ideas. The theory behind brainstorming is that imagination and judgement are two distinct processes. Imagination should be given free reign to produce ideas before judgment is brought onto the scene.

Brainstorming can be done individually or with others. One person should be made responsible for jotting down the ideas. Remember:
- criticism is out;
- freewheeling is welcome — the wilder the better;
- hitchhiking, expanding on others' ideas, is welcome too;
- the more ideas, the better.

Brainstorming should be intensive and take place over an agreed-upon, preset period of time. Once your brainstorming session is complete, give a copy of the list of ideas to everyone in the group. Then begin analyzing and judging them. At a later session, decide which are the best ideas according to your group's needs and priorities. Then polish the final selection.

2

Where are you coming from?

Why citizen involvement?

> *The health of a democratic society may be measured by the quality of functions performed by private citizens.*
> Alexis de Tocqueville

There is no substitute for the *active* responsibility of one citizen for another. Citizens can help people:

Directly   Visiting the sick, caring for children, transporting the disabled, organizing minority groups, etc.

Indirectly   Serving on boards and commissions, influencing political decisions, etc.

Self-help   Alcoholics Anonymous, citizens organizing themselves to change a situation, etc.

Evidence shows private citizen groups have become more dependent on the resources of government, which suggests that government can have control over their programs. People are concerned about this and are asking the following questions:

1. Are citizens abdicating their day-to-day responsibility for each other (and their talents) in favour of professional and other government-financed alternatives? (Professionals should be an *aid*, not a *substitute*.)
2. Do government-financed citizen programs lack the sensitivity and flexibility of a spontaneous community response?

3. Does government involvement undermine citizens' ability to solve their own problems and lead to stagnation and alienation within the community?
4. Is government action more costly than citizen action? Is government taking on a financial burden unnecessarily?

> *Nothing, nothing, nothing, no error, no crime*
> *is so absolutely repugnant to God as everything which*
> *is official; and why? because the official is*
> *so impersonal and therefore the deepest insult which*
> *can be offered to a personality.*
> Soren Kierkegaard

Good Reading

The Management and Fund Raising Centre produces low-cost "how to" information and training workshops in the areas of management and fund raising (resource development). The Centre conducts workshops, writes the weekly newspaper column "Community Alive!," publishes a series of "how to" pamphlets ($1.50 each), "Organizing Your Way to Dollars," which includes such topics as:
- Grant Proposal Checklist;
- News Release Checklist;
- Know Your Printing and Save Money;
- Effective Public Speaking;
- Fund Raising Letters;
- Your Board of Directors;
- How to Budget;
- A Membership Campaign;
- Resource Development Checklist;
- Working with Other Groups;
- Special Fund Raising Events.

The workshops are tailormade to the needs of individual organizations on such topics as:
- The Effective Board;
- Resource Development;
- Government Relations;
- Volunteers;
- Communications (Internal and External);
- Program Planning and Evaluation;
- Management and Administration;
- Paid Personnel.

For more information contact the Centre at:

Management and Fund Raising Centre,
287 MacPherson Avenue,
Toronto, Ontario
M4V 1A4
416-961-0381

Bert Strauss and Mary E. Stowe. *How to Get Things Changed: A Handbook for Tackling Community Problems.* New York: Doubleday and Company, Inc., 1974. This book describes successful methods of involving others in local action. Among the topics covered are:

- eliciting citizen-views of community problems;
- ways of reaching youth;
- planning successful job fairs;
- using educational TV for community communication;
- informing local and state officials;
- planning and conducting conferences.

Appendices include notes on being an effective facilitator, factors of human motivation, conference evaluation and notes on problem solving.

Old timer: one who remembers
when charity was a virtue and
not an organization.
Unknown

Motives for getting involved

He is the best of men who dislikes power.
Mohammed

Most philosophers tell us it is impossible to give without receiving something in return. To bestow an act of kindness usually makes us feel a little better. Nothing wrong with this, but we do need to explore why we want to volunteer our time. Some reasons might be:
- need for acceptance by other people;
- need for friendship;
- stepping stone to something bigger;
- need to feel important and useful.

One researcher drew up an interesting table.* All respondents were asked to give the two main reasons why they were involved with citizen groups.

Categories of Reasons	Number of Times Response Given	Percent of all Respondents (564)
Altruistic	493	87.4
Self-Interest	442	78.4
Sociability	152	27.0
Rational	189	33.5
Religious/ethical	83	14.7
Other	—	—

*Novia Carter. *Volunteers: The Untapped Potential.* The Canadian Council on Social Development, 55 Parkdale Avenue, Ottawa, Ontario K1Y 4G1, 1974.

7

Helping is a two-way street. Don't be condescending, and beware of labelling people. It will limit your understanding of who they really are!

> *Before destruction a man's heart is haughty,*
> *but humility goes before honour.*
> Proverbs 18:12

Good Reading

Esther Stanton. *Clients Come Last: Volunteer and Welfare Organizations.* Beverley Hills, California: Sage Publications, 1970. Discusses the selfishness of service volunteers. A study of the "dramatisation of virtue"—the myths that surround volunteering: "the modern morality play — a civic drama". The book attempts to separate the illusions from the realities of community action. It does not try to identify villains . . . "the people are decent, well-meaning, community-minded individuals trapped in a system which they themselves perpetuate".

Abraham Maslow. *The Farther Reaches of Human Nature.* New York: Viking Press, 1971. Explains what motivates people.

The problem solver as problem seeker

In an American study, a team of six medical doctors examined 400 school children for tonsillitis. They found 80 cases. A second team of six doctors who didn't know another medical team preceded them examined the remaining 320 "healthy" children and diagnosed 63 further cases of tonsilitis.

This procedure was repeated twice more. The end result was that a total of 198 cases were diagnosed—a full 118 more than found by the original medical team. The study, for the most part, ruled out incompetence on the part of the first medical team and concluded that the diagnosing instrument (the doctors) was so biased in favour of finding cases of tonsillitis they couldn't help but diagnose it.

Professionals working with individuals and communities must guard against this problem-seeking bias, even though they have been highly trained to diagnose and solve problems. Similarly, citizen groups and concerned citizens can start expensive and time-consuming action or perpetuate their group's lifespan even when there isn't a problem or reason for their existence. In short, make sure your concern is real, not imagined. (See "Get Your Facts Straight," "The Survey," and "The Research Study," in this chapter.)

8

Taking too much is dangerous

From the outset, citizen groups must guard against situations in which more is being taken than given. Human service groups often attract people who satisfy their own personal needs and confuse this with helping the group, e.g., the board member who relishes the status he thinks the position gives. Self-gratification is important, but not over and above the goals of the group. This is one reason why some human service groups achieve so little, going in ever-increasing circles until they sink. Here are some examples:

1. *The straight loss.* The fund-raising effort costs more in funds and human resources than it creates.
2. *The unmotivated.* A person's expenses are paid so he can attend a meeting, yet that person does not join in the discussions, will not participate in task group work, does not attend regularly.
3. *The inept.* A person (following orientation or training) cannot cope with the job at hand, to the point where others are diverted from their tasks to "prop up" that person.
4. *The overenthusiastic.* A person becomes so emotionally committed that an interim difficulty causes a major frustration, which in turn jeopardizes the long-term goal.
5. *Unhealthy dependency.* A person or group working with a troubled person encourages dependency to the point where the person cannot begin to use his own resources to fend for himself. Presumably this relationship nourishes the needs of the helper!
6. *The learning experience.* Taking too much sometimes is justified if someone is involved because of what he can learn, rather than what he can contribute. However, be careful. Many organizations recruit learners thinking they'll turn into productive workers in no time—*not* usually true. If a person is there to learn, see him from the outset as a person who will use up your existing resources, not the reverse.

The way others see you

Majorities, of course, start with minorities.
Robert Moses

A young man, employed as a youth worker, decided that to help transient young people survive using their own abilities was healthier psychologically and cheaper than encouraging those same young people to be dependent on handouts from a string of social service agencies. At the time, young people were experimenting with alternate

9

lifestyles and concepts of collectivism, sharing their meagre resources and possessions. They did survive, they did learn and they did grow. And the young man was branded a communist!

Why? His actions were highly practical, without any political motivation and saved taxpayers' money. Presumably, by encouraging young people to support themselves, he raised the fear that with this independence, as opposed to the dependence cultivated by the social service agency, the young people might develop into an independent pressure group against the mainstream. His arguments that youth must experiment and grow fell on deaf ears.

Citizen groups and individuals, to their great surprise, may find that their motivations and actions are misinterpreted (sometimes political- ly) when they try to do something they judge helpful to the communi- ty. Before you begin any course of action, think about how it might be perceived by your detractors. Know where you stand and why. Also, know where they stand and why. And remember, the going can be rough — people are afraid of change and new groups.

Coping with opposition

He who slings mud generally loses ground.
Adlai Stevenson

The moment you take a position or action which may affect the in- terests of others, you are almost bound to attract criticism and sometimes organized opposition. This can come from within your own group or from outsiders. There are some general guidelines to deal with this situation.

Be prepared. First, if you've checked out your issue thoroughly, you should have a good idea of the amount of support you can expect. Next, you should place yourself in your opponents' position. Having done this, is there any reason for you to modify *your* position? Will doing so compromise your long-term goal? Can you give in on something that may be a short-term setback, yet will not get in the way of your long-term objectives? Never repel your opponent without let- ting him know that you have considered or will consider his position.

Never lose your cool. If possible, have someone else take over for you when the going gets rough. Make sure you have friends who can support you. While not making light of the issue, try not to take yourself too seriously all the time. Humour is a wonderful way to keep a sense of perspective on yourself and the general situation. If the op- position continues, it makes good sense to leave the battle entirely for a while—go away to a quiet place.

If you simply cannot cope with the stress that a conflict situation creates, then find a replacement and quit your leadership role.

Above all, from the outset understand that *conflict is bound to crop up to some degree* and unless you are prepared to deal with it, you shouldn't take another step forward.

For types of opposition tactics you might use, see Chapter 11 of this manual.

> *Silence is the element in which great things*
> *fashion themselves.*
> Thomas Carlyle

3

Getting started

Inspiration without perspiration is usually sterile.
Unknown

Get your facts straight

Luck, that's when preparation and opportunity meet.
Attributed to Pierre Elliott Trudeau

Once you decide your issue is worth pursuing, it is important that you find out if your perception of the need is correct. To do this, you need to know what's really going on. You must conduct a thorough review of the information available in your area. This is time-consuming, but it will pay off in the end.

Complete information is the raw material you will use to create a plan that will succeed in making your aims real. You will use it to:
- write a convincing brief;
- persuade the public to give you support;
- fight opposition, etc.

Remember, knowledge is power.

Don't reinvent the wheel! Find out if what you want to do has been done before.

Where to go
Before using a library, make an appointment with the librarian to discuss your needs and library services available.

1. *Public libraries* lend books. Through inter-library loans, you can borrow books from other libraries in your city or state. Large municipal libraries often have important specialized collections. A reference librarian can steer you to the information you need.

2. *Colleges and universities* have large general library collections and usually several specialized collections. Professors and research people may be remarkably well informed about the problem you are trying to solve. Check an index of dissertation abstracts in the library for unpublished research.

3. *Corporations and businesses* often have specialized libraries open to the public.

4. *Federal Information Centers* maintain libraries of government publications and provide information about the whole range of federal agencies and programs. The Centers are generally located in federal office buildings in large cities, but may be called toll-free from certain other cities in the same state. See the *United States Government Manual*, available at your local library, for a complete list of FICs and a description of the range of information services they provide.

5. *Government depository libraries*, located in large public and university libraries, have vast holdings of federal publications and documents. A list of government depository libraries can be ordered from the Chief of the Library, Department of Public Documents, U.S. Government Printing Office, Washington, D.C. 20402.

6. *Newspaper clipping libraries* are usually found at large newspapers only. All clippings are arranged under subject headings. Check beforehand to see if there is a charge for use.

7. *Film libraries* in larger municipal library systems lend films and have catalogues with film descriptions and reviews. They also rent projectors and teach how to use them. Governments lend films, film strips, slides and video tapes. Consult the *Audio-Visual Catalog Director*, published by the National Audio-Visual Center, National Archives and Record Services, General Services Administration, Washington, D.C. 20409, for descriptions of federal film holdings and distribution arrangements. See also the *Guide to State Loan Films*, Serina Press, 70 Kennedy Street, Alexandria, Virginia 22305.

8. *Associations* may be able to give you information about your area of concern. There are tens of thousands of nonprofit associations in the United States; the names and addresses of 17,000 can be

found in the *Encyclopedia of Associations*, Gale Research Company, Book Tower, Detroit, Michigan 48226.

9. *Community information centres* dispense information about citizen groups, local government, and available resources and their location. They are also involved with identifying community needs, and provide translation and interpreter services.

10. *National and international banks of information* can be tapped (this is called information retrieval) by using a computer terminal. You can usually find this in a library or a university.

11. *Government departments* (local, county, state and federal) may know a lot about your area of concern. Contact an information officer.

12. *A church or ecumenical council* (a co-ordinating group of churches) can give general advice if it is active in local social issues.

13. *Other community groups* can be your closest allies. Not only do they have inexhaustible quantities of local experience, they can give you support and direction. Also contact interagency councils, special interest coalitions and other umbrella organizations.

It is not good for a man to be without knowledge,
and he who makes haste with his feet misses his way.
Proverbs 19:2

A good all-around reference book is the current *Information Please Almanac* (New York: Simon and Schuster), available in all libraries. It includes listings of:
- federal executive departments and agencies;
- academic institutions;
- courts and judges;
- churches and religious organizations;
- museums and art galleries;
- libraries;
- newspapers and magazines;
- labour unions;
- leading foundations;
- societies and associations;
- incumbent senators and congressmen.

Search out all available information. Don't duplicate an existing program if you can strengthen it by joining. Getting information is the best way of meeting people who can help you achieve your goal. Keep up these contacts.

When approaching any group or organization new to you, start at the top (the president, the director). They may refer you down the line but at least they'll know you exist. And follow up your conversation with a note confirming what was said. Courtesy pays. (If the person you speak with refers you to others, send a carbon copy of the note to them, too.)

The first meeting

To lead people, you must follow behind.
Lao Tsu

It's people who count. Everyone you meet as you make your dream real is potentially a member of either your base of support in the community or your network of contacts for resources and new information. It is the individuals associated with organizations who can help you, not the organizations by themselves! No matter how busy you are, take the time to know these people. In the long run, they are your most important resource.

Once you have satisfied yourself that an issue in your community needs a new group to cope with it you must begin to find people to help you. Invite a small group of people (six to ten) to discuss the issue further. They should:

- know the community;
- be interested in the problem;
- be able to evaluate the issue (generally);
- be able to seek out their own information.

Some of these people should be from other citizen groups. It is important to co-ordinate your efforts with other groups in your community.

Meetings are for one or more of the following purposes:

- sharing information;
- getting new ideas and insights;
- making decisions;
- dividing workload
- building morale.

16

Always have an agenda (a detailed plan for the meeting, with background information if possible). Make sure everyone agrees with it before you start. After discussion, ask each person the questions you've already asked yourself. You'll be surprised at the varied responses. Take notes on what is said (the minutes) and send them out after the meeting to the people who attended.

Tip: It is a good idea to put yourself in a postion of serving the people who come to your meeting, e.g., taking their coats, offering refreshments. This helps calm their anxiety about your "taking over."

It often helps to know how *not* to be successful. The following excerpt from an article by Laird O'Brien shows how one group avoided learning the hard way!

How to sabotage a meeting without really trying

BY R. LAIRD O'BRIEN

AT 9:05 A.M., Bob Wiele opened the meeting by saying, "Let's take 20 minutes to draw up a list of all the things we can do to make sure this meeting will be totally unproductive and useless."

Nervous laughter. Scraping of chairs. The 20 people in the room had been drawn together from different backgrounds, jobs and communities to design a major plan of action. Not an easy day's work. And they weren't expecting that Bob Wiele, an adult education leader brought in for the day, would start them off with games.

Twenty minutes later they reconvened and Bob started writing their "sabotage list" as he called it, on a flip chart. Page after page of verbal grenades. Here they are, with a few comments and examples added:

(1) Stick to the social niceties. Keep it all polite, friendly, non-combative. Don't get your image dirty.

(2) Argue over format instead of the problem. Hours can be swallowed up in debating who should speak first, who should take notes, when to break for lunch, who pays

(3) Don't get involved. Maintain a posture of spectator, foreigner, outsider —someone who has stumbled in by accident.

(4) Keep saying, "We've still got plenty of time." This encourages background excursions, coffee-breaks, jokes, lunch-breaks, irrelevant examples.

(5) Toss in bizarre remarks. "Damn that fly. I'm going to get him—Whack!—before this day is over!" Whack! "When are we going to break for lunch?" Whack! "Why did we pick this hotel?" Whack!

(6) Let three or four dominate the meeting.

(7) Have not enough leadership, or too much. A meeting can wander aimlessly up and down blind alleys, around in circles and disperse in darkness. Equally disastrous is the one that walks a tightrope, stifling all exploratory ideas and questions.

(8) Don't clarify the issue. A superficial outline usually guarantees a superficial discussion.

(9) Settle for a consensus instead of a decision.

(10) Refuse to think nationally ("My people won't go for it!").

(11) Lie. Say one thing, but don't mean it—so there will be absolutely no follow-through.

(12) Criticize but don't offer alternatives.

(13) Cry, poor me. Often.

(14) Close the mind. Keep saying, "It won't work." "I never heard of such a thing." "We tried that before." Don't let any fresh ideas sneak in.

(15) Detail it to death. Get down to the nitty-gritty of where you'll rent the desk that the man you plan to hire will sit behind.

There you have one group's guide as to why meetings may flounder. (Not just meetings either.)

By 9:50 p.m. that night, when the meeting finally broke up, every one of the points on the sabotage list had actually been attempted by someone. But dragging the possibilities out early, holding them up to the light and laughing at them, all help to pull a group together to a task, and also help them to recognize and quickly pounce on saboteurs when they do start their dirty work

(Reprinted with permission from *The Globe and Mail*)

Good Reading

P.G. Green. *Getting People Together*. Community Development Branch, Ministry of Community and Social Services, 3rd Floor, Hepburn Block Toronto, Ontario M7A 1E9. An excellent guide, essential reading for a new group. The book looks at:

- getting a citizen group together;
- defining its purpose;
- planning your first public meeting;
- adjustments under crisis conditions;
- when to quit;
- structure — yes or no?;
- involving more people;
- relationships with other groups.

Lawrence Wilford Bridge. *The Funk and Wagnalls Book of Parliamentary Procedure*. New York: Funk and Wagnalls, 1954. A complete explanation of parliamentary procedure with charts, samples and model forms for specific actions such as motions, minutes and reports. The book also describes the roles and functions of boards and committees and offers advice on planning and holding mass meetings and conventions. It concludes with "scripts" of six model business meetings.

Mrs. Harry Harvey Thomas. *Simplified Parliamentary Procedure*. League of Women Voters, 1730 M Street, N.W., Washington, D.C. 20036. 12 pp. 15¢. This pamphlet is based on Robert's Rules of Order.

Donald R. Fessler. *Meetings That Get Results*. Blacksburg, Virginia: Community Training Associates, Inc., 1971.

19

How to Conduct a Meeting. New York: The Dun and Bradstreet Business Library, Apollo Editions, 1969.

Audrey R. Trecker and Harleigh B. Trecker. *Committee Common Sense.* New York: Whiteside, Inc. and William Morrow & Company, Inc., 1954.

> *We seldom repent talking too little,*
> *but very often talking too much.*
> Jean de la Bruyere

The public meeting

> *A great many people think they are thinking when*
> *they are merely rearranging their prejudices.*
> William James

After the first meeting of a core of interested citizens has been held, it is time to solicit wider community involvement. The following sections outline the various methods of doing this.

The public meeting is one way of finding out more about the problem or issue your group is interested in and usually lasts for two to three hours. It also involves your community and gets people's support for your efforts. Public meetings consist of two-way communication. You explain the problem; people give facts, their experiences, opinions and advice. Then, based on this new information, you explain a plan of action and people say whether they think it will work.

The following points may help in planning your group's public meeting.

1. *Make sure people know about your meeting.*Send a press release (see Section A, Chapter 10 of this manual) to local newspapers, radio stations, etc. Put up posters or pass out leaflets door-to-door. Make sure you present the purpose of your meeting in an interesting way. P.G. Green in his book, *Getting People Together,* points out:

   "It is no longer enough to reserve a hall, stick a notice on a lamppost and wait for everyone to arrive. Your first meeting must have particularly careful planning and publicity. Ask yourself as an outsider: 'Would I go to that meeting? Who's holding it? What for? Is it worth paying a babysitter?' "

2. *Hold your meeting on a weekday evening,* and check to see it won't be competing with another important event. Try to find a well-ventilated room with comfortable seats, donated free (see Chapter 6 on Resource Development,)

20

3. *Select a leader (chairperson) for your meeting with great care.* This person should be friendly, tactful, patient, neutral, able to guide discussion so it stays on topic and doesn't drag, able to co-ordinate the various points of view. He should learn as much as possible about the subject to be discussed.
4. *Start your meeting with a written background,* clearly stating the issue: why you are calling the meeting or starting your group.
5. *What do you want from the public meeting?* Do other people see your problem as real? More information about the problem? Ideas for solving it? People's support for your group? Volunteers? Plan your meeting accordingly.
6. *Make your subject specific enough* that some decisions can be reached, and not so broad that people become overwhelmed.
7. *Keep your meeting short and to the point.* One to two hours is long enough.
8. *Take notes* on important points of the discussion.
9. *Always be guided by what comes out of the meeting.* If you go your own way, you will lose community support.
10. *Make sure everyone understands what has been decided* and what your group plans to do next before closing the meeting. Always set a date — even if approximate — for a follow-up.
11. *Try to have refreshments after the meeting.* People will get to know each other and may become members of your group.
12. *Beware of special interest groups* who seek to pack an open meeting — and with their "majority" push something on your community that is not wanted by the real majority of involved citizens.

Follow-up makes the difference between action and more hot air. Be sure to get everyone's name, address and telephone number. Send a report of the meeting to everyone who attended as well as notices of further meetings. If people volunteer to do things, check to see if they are doing what they said they would.

Good Reading
Discussion Leaders' Handbook. Ontario Ministry of Culture and Recreation, c/o Ontario Government Bookstore, 880 Bay Street, Toronto, Ontario M7A 1N8. 50¢.

Richard Beckhard. *How to Plan and Conduct Workshops and Conferences.* New York: Association Press (Leadership Library Series). $1.00. Explains initial planning, fact finding and evaluation, program development, conference planning and preparation, record taking and follow-up action.

Rachel Dubois and Mew-Soong Li. *The Art of Group Conversation*. New York: Association Press, 1963. Tested ways to break through mistrust, prejudice, cultural and ethnic differences, language difficulties, class and other barriers to group co-operation.

The community conference

People can share in making decisions about their community by attending a community conference. This type of gathering usually lasts a minimum of one day.

Its purpose is to come up with a specific plan or solution to an issue or problem. It goes into more detail than is possible in a public meeting and has the following advantages:
- It taps a broad cross section of opinion and insight, and often reveals new information.
- It informs and stimulates the participants.
- People have the feeling they belong to a community and are partners in its development.
- Several plans to solve a problem can be evaluated.
- A broad-based consensus is reached on how to cope with a common problem.

After the talking is over, get a specific commitment *in writing* from as many people as possible. A follow-up committee must check on each person's progress if the work is to get done.

The teach-in is another version of the community conference, the difference being that it convenes a series of workshops to teach skills to citizens. The organization is the same as for the community conference. A combination of the community conference and the teach-in is the most useful approach.

The diagram below shows how to plan a community conference.

Planning the conference

Each subcommittee chairperson usually selects those who serve on his subcommittee.

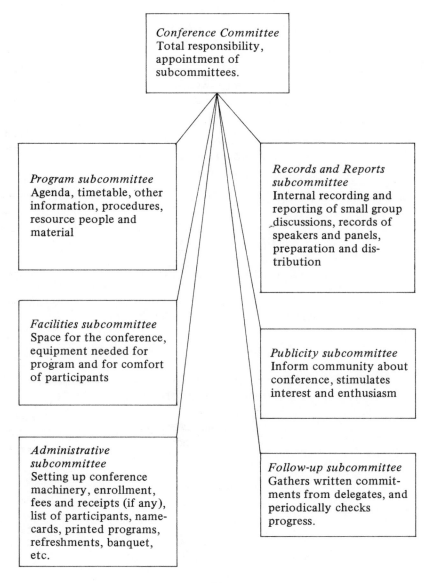

Conference Committee
Total responsibility,
appointment of
subcommittees.

Program subcommittee
Agenda, timetable, other
information, procedures,
resource people and
material

Records and Reports
subcommittee
Internal recording and
reporting of small group
discussions, records of
speakers and panels,
preparation and dis-
tribution

Facilities subcommittee
Space for the conference,
equipment needed for
program and for comfort
of participants

Publicity subcommittee
Inform community about
conference, stimulates
interest and enthusiasm

Administrative
subcommittee
Setting up conference
machinery, enrollment,
fees and receipts (if any),
list of participants, name-
cards, printed programs,
refreshments, banquet,
etc.

Follow-up subcommittee
Gathers written commit-
ments from delegates, and
periodically checks
progress.

The conference in action

The idea
tested and recommended
by the initiating group

The conference committee
plans and arranges

Plenary session
informs, orients, stimulates
all participants

Small groups
study, discussion, opinions, report

Small Group A   Small Group B   Small Group C

Plenary Session
reports from small groups
(co-ordinated and total opinion expressed)

Appoints action follow-up committee

Obtains a commitment for action from all participants

Conference report
reviews, selects, arranges, interprets
in concise, dynamic form

distribution to

General public
Action follow-up committee checks progress

Good Reading

W. Warner Burke and Richard Beckhard. *Conference Planning,* University Associates, 7596 Eads Avenue, La Jolla, California 92037, 1976 (2nd ed.).

Leonard Nadler and Zeace Nadler. *The Conference Book.* Gulf Publishing Company, P.O. Box 2608, Houston, Texas 77001, 1977. A complete guide to designing and conducting conferences.

The survey

The future not being born, my friend,
we will abstain from baptizing it.
George Meredith

A well-organized survey gathers many different opinions and shows how an issue or problem is viewed by people in the community. A good survey has:
- a carefully planned questionnaire;
- a wide range of persons and organizations to be contacted.

(If possible, find someone skilled to develop these, e.g., a researcher.)

Staff members of a university or other institution of further education can help you develop a survey. In addition, they can provide students to carry out the survey. An advertising agency or market research firm may also be able to help. (See Chapter 6 on Resource Development.)

The person-to-person interview is the most effective way of conducting a survey. A mailing usually has a small return. An alternative is to follow up a mailing with a telephone call to each person.

Many people will not divulge personal information unless they like and trust the interviewer. Therefore, the interviewer must inspire confidence. The interviewee should be told what the survey is about and that he has been selected randomly and is representing many others. If a person is unwilling to answer a question, the interviewer should respect his privacy and go on to the next question. Always remember, the interviewee receives no payment for his effort.

You might try recording opinions using a tape recorder or video machine. This material, when edited, is an excellent accompaniment to your questionnaire findings when making a presentation for community or political support or resources.

Good Reading
Rowland Warren. *Studying Your Community.* Free Press, 1965. Covers all aspects of surveying and research. Chapter 18, "Organizing a Community Survey," covers different kinds and uses of survey, the steps in a citizen survey, and human relations in survey work. Chapter 19, "Aids to the Survey," gives guidance on interviewing and using a questionnaire.

The research study

What is research but a blind date with knowledge?
Will Harvey

A properly designed research study is an immense undertaking. It sets out to measure, in depth and objectively, all aspects of an issue or problem. Great care should be taken to find out whether other options are available, such as the survey. Here are some questions to ask yourself:

- Are you sure that identical or similar research information does not already exist? Consult the indexes to dissertation abstracts in a college library. Check *Metropolitan Surveys*, an annual listing of recent community surveys and research projects; free from the School of Public Affairs, State University of New York, 179 Partridge St., Albany, N.Y. 12203. Or see *Science Research in Progress*, listing 125,000 current projects.
- Did your search for other research material go back at least five years and include research in other countries?

If you decide to proceed with a research study, check to see if a qualified person nearby will carry out the study for free. Examples are people in a government department, university or market research company. If not, find research professionals to help you write a brief asking for money to enable hiring a person or group to carry out the research project. (For information on where to submit your brief, see Chapter 6.)

Once your study is complete, others usually see you as having special, perhaps invaluable, information about the issue or problem, and you become able to influence opinion and policy in this area. (See "The Lobby," Chapter 11.) This strategic consideration is a major "plus" for doing a research study.

Remember, it's easier to study something than to roll up your sleeves and do something about it. Don't get caught studying a problem to death.

There are three kinds of lies:
lies, damned lies and statistics.
Benjamin Disraeli

The demonstration project

To avoid criticism,
do nothing, say nothing, be nothing.
Elbert Hubbard

A demonstration project tests a plan of action. It is the action equivalent of a study—a fascinating combination of research, survey, community involvement and direct action. Simply stated it is a trial-and-error approach. A demonstration project tests either a completely new and untried approach to a particular problem, or an already tried method (changed to meet your needs).

Usually the demonstration project is short-lived. It must be kept under a formal and continual review. A group of citizens, including knowledgeable professionals, can do this and suggest needed changes. Involve other organizations, particularly if you may ask them to continue the project on a year-round basis. If your project has staff, it too should participate in any evaluation. Keep a good record of your project's activities and your evaluation. You will use it for any continuation of the project.

When an approach works, the options are:

1. to continue the demonstration for a limited time until the issue or problem is solved;
2. to convert the demonstration into a year-round program;
3. to pass on what you've learned to an already established organization so they can continue the approach (see "The Lobby" and "The Parallel Institution," in Chapter 11).

If your demonstration project fails, or the need lessens, don't hesitate to "close up shop."

Beware of letting your project be used as a token (band-aid) solution to appease current public concern, only to be dropped later when it really is needed.

Research and demonstration grants are offered by all levels of government and by the private sector as well. Consult the *Annual Register of Grant Support*, available at your library.

27

The task force

As the name implies, the citizen task force carries out specific tasks and organizes new citizen groups quickly. It is a high expenditure of energy over a short period—like the 100-metre dash! The short-term (anything from a week to six months), high-output nature of the task force makes it an effective body for starting or changing something. It is not appropriate for administering the long-term activities of a project or program.

People who work on task forces must be action-oriented ("do-it" types), well organized and able to meet schedules. A task force, because it is short and to the point, is especially appealing to busy people. Once the task force's objectives are achieved, it is disbanded.

The coalition

The coalition is made up of several groups and individuals involved with an issue or problem. Members usually gather, at least for the first time, around a particular and immediate situation.

Thus, the coalition is an effective way to:
• draw together autonomous (independent) groups;
• survey an issue from different viewpoints;
• plan and launch action.

By planning and working together, separate groups are informally co-ordinating their activities. This broadens the base of support and gives the coalition additional impact when advocating a particular position. Once the original situation is dealt with, a coalition can go on to play an important ongoing planning and co-ordinating role in the community (see Chapter 12.)

The coalition is unique in that it protects the autonomy of the groups. It is a useful unifying tool for organizations working in the same field who want to form an umbrella or co-ordinating organization, but don't want to incorporate a new organization with its hassles about constitutional representation on a board, etc.

published by Kids Can Press, P.O. Box 5974 Station A, Toronto © Ann Weatherby, 1971

Good Reading

Malcolm Shookner. *Human Service Networks and Coalitions.* Human Services Study Group, Goddard College, Plainfield, Vermont, 1976. Describes coalitions in considerable detail. This study, carried out in Canada, is the most comprehensive of its type in North America.

4

Your group's structure

The loosely structured citizen group

> *The world is moving so fast these days*
> *that the man who says it can't be done*
> *is generally interrupted by someone doing it.*
> Elbert Hubbard

Most citizen groups start spontaneously in reaction to a local situation. Many do not approve of the conventional organization with a board of directors, standing committees, etc. Rather, everyone joins in and shares responsibilities equally. A "collective" sense prevails.

The members of the small citizen group usually set policy and carry out the programs ("operations"). Such groups usually do not hire staff. If such a group must incorporate to receive funds or to legitimize itself, it tends to meet minimum legal requirements (for board members and officers) "on paper" rather than in a working sense. The group can have various work sub-groups to avoid wearing out those involved with the main programs.

The totally unstructured group is dangerous because:
- no one is really accountable or finally responsible for any tasks;
- anyone can handle the group's money;
- there is no formal way of settling arguments within the group;
- people end up going in different directions because there is no leadership or general control.

31

Good Reading

P.G. Green. *Getting People Together.* (See page 19 of this manual for more information.)

The incorporated organization

Don't let your status become too quo!
Unknown

Organizational structure ranges between the "vertical" (chain of command from top to bottom) and the "horizontal" or "open" (where all members of the group are equal). Conventional organizations lean toward the vertical, with a predetermined "pecking order."

"Organizations are pervasively described these days as too impersonal, too big, as being beyond control by mere mortals. They are even seen by some as monsters which man has created but which seem to have acquired wills of their own. The antidote to this type of thinking is to better understand organizations as tools to serve man's individual and collective purposes."

Paul R. Lawrence and Jay W. Lorsch, *Developing Organizations: Diagnosis and Action* (Reading, Massachusetts: Addison-Wesley, 1969).

". . . (Organizations are) widely criticized for not possessing the ability to change, riddled with excessive overhead, inefficiency, waste and general rigidity. A cynic would suggest that no corporate or charitable organization ever really reforms itself. While some reform programs may be good, other will be window dressing designed to keep the cash flow coming in!"

Novia Carter, "Trends in Voluntary Support for Non-government Social Service Agencies" (Canadian Council on Social Development, 1974).

"Agencies have to change into flexible organizations practically without a performance policy, prepare to switch the work process and, if necessary, change their structure so as to enable the solution of new problems and the satisfaction of new needs in the rapidly changing community."

J.W. Frei, "The Executive and His Role in Social Services" (Social Planning Council of Metropolitan Toronto, 1974.)

"Western institutions are reactive. This is to say, they are conceived at the last possible minute before a minor problem threatens to become a major one. In future, our planning must include the building of preventive or positive institutions."

John Fisher

Why incorporate

Incorporation helps a community group when it wants to:
- show stability and responsibility—incorporation is one more step toward permanency;
- limit its liability (for debt, etc.);
- remain in operation over a period of years;
- commit itself (legally) to written objectives (the "objects" clause in corporation papers);
- obtain funds from government and foundations (many refuse to fund unincorporated groups);
- qualify as a tax-exempt organization for federal and state income tax purposes. It is not *necessary* to incorporate in order to acquire tax-exempt status, but it may facilitate the application process. Before the Internal Revenue Service will grant an exemption, it must be convinced that your group is organized on a solid basis; incorporation may help your credibility.

An egghead is one who stands firmly
on both feet, in mid-air, on both
sides of an issue.
Homer Ferguson

Why not to incorporate

- Small groups may attach themselves to another organization, and use its support services and incorporated status. This arrangement must not limit the independence of the group.
- Incorporation opens all your records and documents to scrutiny by both the IRS and the state that issued your charter.
- An incorporated group may be more likely than a less formal association to attract the wrong sort of attention — lawsuits, for example. While incorporation preserves the members of your organization from personal liability, it makes the organization as a whole responsible for the actions of any one of its members or employees. A serious error or indiscretion on the part of single member, if performed in the course of his duties on behalf of the organization, could threaten the corporation's assets and legal position. It is worth noting that most labour unions are not incorporated.

SAMPLE CONFIGURATION OF A TYPICAL NONPROFIT ORGANIZATION

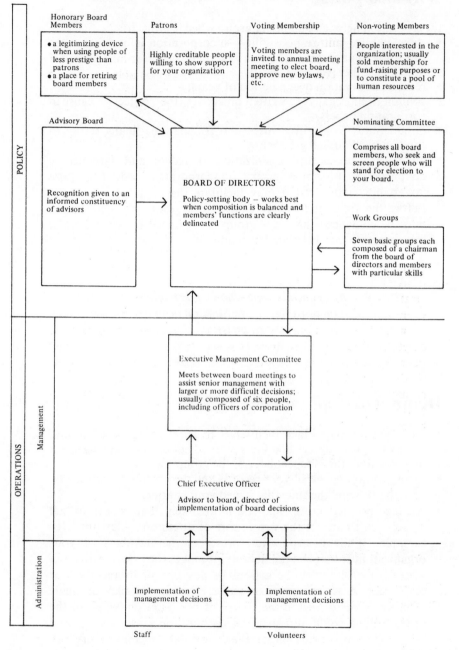

Honorary Board Members
- a legitimizing device when using people of less prestige than patrons
- a place for retiring board members

Patrons
Highly creditable people willing to show support for your organization

Voting Membership
Voting members are invited to annual meeting meeting to elect board, approve new bylaws, etc.

Non-voting Members
People interested in the organization; usually sold membership for fund-raising purposes or to constitute a pool of human resources

Advisory Board
Recognition given to an informed constituency of advisors

BOARD OF DIRECTORS
Policy-setting body — works best when composition is balanced and members' functions are clearly delineated

Nominating Committee
Comprises all board members, who seek and screen people who will stand for election to your board.

Work Groups
Seven basic groups each composed of a chairman from the board of directors and members with particular skills

Executive Management Committee
Meets between board meetings to assist senior management with larger or more difficult decisions; usually composed of six people, including officers of corporation

Chief Executive Officer
Advisor to board, director of implementation of board decisions

Implementation of management decisions

Implementation of management decisions

Staff

Volunteers

POLICY

OPERATIONS

Management

Administration

34

Steps to incorporation

1. Appoint a committee.
2. Get a lawyer. You may find one willing to volunteer his services; if not, your local community legal service might be able to provide the help you need at a low price. In any case, it is important to have a lawyer with experience in nonprofit law. Go to an established nonprofit organization and ask the name of its lawyer. Legal fees for incorporation can range from as little as $50 to as much as $300.
3. Borrow photocopies of similar organizations' incorporation papers—their constitutions and bylaws.
4. Obtain the necessary application forms and a copy of the act governing nonprofit corporations in your state. In most states you would write to the office of the secretary of state. Incorporation in one state does not restrict your activities to that state; you may operate more or less freely anywhere in the country—subject to local laws. State filing fees range from $20 to $80.
5. Draft a constitution and a set of bylaws. Bylaws are the rules that govern your organization. Although most groups are given "boiler plate" (standard) bylaws by their lawyers, these must be carefully checked. They are not law unless formally accepted by your organization. A resolution by the board of directors, ratified by the organization's voting members, can change any bylaw. An annual bylaw review should be implemented to ensure that all bylaws meet your current needs. Make sure your bylaws are in harmony with state laws regarding nonprofit corporations.

> *We are not a loved organization,*
> *but we are a respected one.*
> John Fisher

Applying for a tax exemption

Whether your group incorporates or not, it is necessary to apply to the Internal Revenue Service if you want a tax exemption. Incorporation does *not* automatically register your group with the IRS.

An organization's eligibility for federal income tax exemption depends upon the nature of its activities. Groups established for "religious, charitable, educational, scientific, or literary purposes, or to prevent cruelty to children or animals" enjoy a double privilege: they are themselves exempt from income taxes, and donors may deduct their contributions to such groups from personal or corporate income. Under the 1976 Tax Reform Act, public charities are permitted to engage in lobbying, but the amount they may spend on lobbying activities is limited to a percentage of their total exempt purposes expenditures. For example, a group whose expenditures in any one year are less than $500,000 may apply no more than 20 percent of this amount to lobbying. The allowable percentage drops as expenditures rise above $500,000.

A second category of exempt organizations includes labour unions, social clubs, and organizations dedicated to "social welfare." It covers all groups whose sole or major activity is the promotion of changes in legislation or government policy. If your group falls within this category, its income may be exempted from taxes, but the people who provide it may not deduct their contributions.

Requirements for exemption from state income taxes generally follow the federal pattern. In many states exemption from state sales taxes are available to nonprofit organizations. Contact your state information office or the office of your secretary of state for details.

Your first step toward securing an exemption should be to obtain a copy of IRS Publication #557, *How to Apply for Recognition of Exemption for an Organization*, available from all IRS Centers.

What is a board of directors?

A board of directors is simply a formal policy-setting group. It is also called "board of governors," which is a more prestigious title used by older, more established organizations.

Why have a board of directors?

All board members can be held liable for the group or organization (depending on circumstances — the law is complex on this matter), and their reputations are at stake. This is reassuring to outsiders who do business with your group or who are donating resources.

Legally, an incorporated organization must have a minimum number of directors. They must assume certain official positions, i.e., president, secretary, treasurer. This varies across the country, so check with your state government.

What are a board of directors' responsibilities?

Primarily, boards set policies used to meet the purpose or goal of an organization. Policies are the rules that embody the intentions of the group. In an incorporated organization, the board is legally responsible for upholding the constitution and bylaws. Also, the board decides who is responsible for what within the organization and how the organization should conduct itself in the community.

In a small group that does not have staff, the policymakers (the board of directors) are also the program workers.

When a group has staff, the policymakers do not have direct responsibility for operations or programs. Instead, they approve or reject major suggestions made by staff. Board members may work with staff people or advise them. It is important, however, that they give up any notions of being in charge when they cross from the policy to the operations area. Here they work for and with staff.

Patience: a minor form of despair
distinguished as a virtue.
Ambrose Bierce

Composition of a board of directors

Although the composition of a board of directors depends on the purpose of the organization, it can include the following:
- representation from different social, economic and cultural groups involved with the problem or issue your group is facing;
- representation from geographic areas;
- client representation, if it's a service organization, or representation by those who are affected in any way by the issue in question if it's a citizens' rights group;
- professional or expert representation in the problem area;
- a balance of men and women;
- lawyer, an accountant and other professionals;
- prestige persons, preferably those who are prepared to work. These could also be invited to join your advisory board.

In general you should follow these guidelines when setting up a board of directors:
1. If you are a citizen group, make sure lay citizens outnumber professional representation by at least two thirds.

37

2. Make sure that your board doesn't engage in token representation: people who are barely interested and who don't show up for board meetings.

People representing an important minority group, who are intimidated by the board process, should be made aware of board procedures and the importance of their participation. Support these people in any way possible.

3. If your group is helping a minority group, but is not governed by a majority of persons from that group, then you must rethink your involvement. The minority group should not simply be "represented" on your board of directors. Instead, you should urge them to start their own organization. Or give them yours — everyone on your board resigns, except for people from the minority group. (Organizations make great presents!) The principle is self-determination. Communities, from the outset, must be responsible for their own well-being — not be dependent on outside help.

A board of directors' recruitment

A board of directors should always be on the lookout for talented, committed and interested people.

For some reason, we don't think of board members as working volunteers — they're something apart. Look at the recruitment strategies for volunteers, Chapter 8. Consider using these to recruit board members. Selecting board members from the ranks of your volunteers, e.g., work groups, standing committees, task groups and direct service people, is one way to reduce "performance risk" (i.e., you have already seen them in action).

Some organizations use their volunteers rather like a hockey team uses a farm team — to develop and evaluate talent! While this is an excellent technique, don't allow it to undermine the representative (communitywide) nature of your board. Also, don't let it exclude new people who may bring fresh energy and ideas to your group.

Board members' orientation or training

All people recruited to a policymaking group (a board of directors) should be well oriented to your organization before they take on their responsibilities. This might be done on a weekend or one evening a week for three or four weeks. Subjects for discussion are:

- need for the organization;
- goals;
- history;
- achievements to date;
- failures;
- current programs;
- future programs;
- current problems;
- responsibilities of board members;
- organization structure;
- difference between policy and operations and how they relate to each other;
- how work groups relate to the full board, and division of labour among the board;
- how board members interact with operations and professional staff;
- how the board can measure the progress of the organization;
- important constituencies of the organization and how the board stays in touch with them;
- reading this manual.

An added benefit of this type of training is that board members get to know one another. This is an important consideration.

All this may seem elementary, but most board members, particularly of larger organizations, spend their first year in a state nearing total confusion. A training program for the policymaking group is a *must* for all organizations, large or small, formally or informally structured.

Have your board divide itself into the seven basic work groups as suggested in this manual, Part II, Introduction.

> *The world is full of people who have never,*
> *since childhood, met an open doorway with*
> *an open mind.*
> E.B. White

Rubberstamp or working unit?

According to time-worn precedent, a board of directors was made up of prestigious, respectable persons who had a general concern for charitable causes. They met, at the most monthly, and rubberstamped the recommendations of a staff. They were a figurehead board, and knew little about the actual workings of the organization. This group was effective only as long as its reputation meant a good deal to those providing financial and other support.

Nowadays, organizations are facing very complex issues. They need all the able people they can muster. The current trend is toward a board consisting of a well-trained, highly involved group of volunteers. The members of this board are an additional working support for the organization. In short the relationship between board and staff is a "working partnership."

A yawn is a silent shout.
G.K. Chesterton

Individual board member responsibilities
Board members must have a good idea what is expected of them individually. All board members must have a job description. This should include such things as representing a point of view or an area of a community, if this is the reason they were appointed. Their responsibilities with standing committees (or as we'll call them, "work groups") should be added. At least twice a year a "round robin" session of the board should evaluate individual contributions in relation to each person's job description. The executive of the board should discuss this evaluation in private and take positive action in areas of weakness.

Election versus appointments
Wherever possible, promote a competition for official positions on your board. An election encourages potential officers to state clearly what they want to achieve. At the halfway point and at year-end, the winning candidates' performance can then be measured against his promises. This system is superior to a passive "nomination slate" where people tend to occupy a position (static), not fulfill a mandate (active).

An executive committee
The executive is a small group of board members including the officers who sit between board meetings. It advises staff and makes decisions on behalf of the board which are not policy; e.g., an unusually large expenditure, a schedule change in a program, etc.

Staff vote
An executive director or equivalent staff person advises policymaking. He should be considered a full participating member of the policymaking group, in an advisory sense (without voting privileges). In this sense, the nonprofit organization should emulate the free enter-

prise organization, which usually permits its chief executive officer to sit as a full member of the board.

The meeting place

Board meetings should take place in front of the progress chart on p. 122. This suggests meeting at your group's office. The chairs may be less comfortable, but it's guaranteed to keep board members in closer touch with operations and save you a bundle in meeting room rental and meal costs. Another tip: coffee puts people on edge. Try tea, fruit juice or milk next time!

> *A prig is a fellow who is always making*
> *you a present of his opinions.*
> George Eliot

Attendance

Have your bylaws state that anyone who can't show good cause must resign if he misses three consecutive board meetings.

Staff attendance

Don't be a boardroom snob. *All* staff, including clerical, should have an open, ongoing invitation to attend board meetings. Include this in your bylaws. This invitation can be withdrawn if staff members are urgently needed elsewhere, or if a matter concerning staff is being discussed.

Parliamentary procedure

At the board orientation session, make sure everyone understands how to run a meeting. Because people are volunteering their time, a board meeting must be crisp and well-organized. It is only for limited discussion and decisions — detailed work should be carried out in committee, and only recommendations are submitted to the board for disciplined discussion and the vote.

Minutes

One person who is not a board member should take minutes (notes) of each meeting. These should include date, time and place of meeting, who is present, main points arising in discussion of each item on the agenda and who stated them, any decisions reached, time of adjournment, and date, time and place of next meeting. These minutes should be distributed to all members of the board and to staff of your group.

41

Telephone conferences

Busy volunteers, boards, work groups and task groups can save time and money by linking up on the telephone. Nobody has to leave his place of work and decisions are reached faster by up to six (recommended maximum) persons meeting on the phone. Call your phone company conference operator two days in advance to book the conference call.

Board member expenses

All board members should be allowed expenses *if needed*. Ask each member at the beginning what expenses he cannot cover. You may be surprised at those who will pay their own way or be able to charge it to their company. If you are a national or statewide organization and people travel long distances to board meetings try to organize car pools or group travel rates on buses or aircraft. Also, to save hotel expenses, try to arrange a billeting system in homes in the town where the board meeting is held. This type of cost-saving can be promoted to your funding sources; it will stand you in good stead while realizing valuable savings.

Duration of board member appointments

Each board member should serve a three-year term, with an annual turn-over of one-third of the membership. Under this arrangement a board member spends his first year orienting himself and learning from senior members, so that in his second year he will be able to assume a high degree of responsibility on the basis of a thorough understanding of the issues. The third year allows him to hand over some responsibilities while giving continuity to the board and counsel to its less experienced members.

To stay youthful, stay useful.
Unknown

Time to retire

A board of directors can become a habit. Sometimes a board accommodates someone who has made invaluable contributions, but is no longer doing so. Don't be cruel — we all become tired after a time! However, remedy the situation by changing your bylaws to state that the maximum time someone can serve as a board member is two or three years. For special contributors who won't retire, amend your bylaws to include an honorary board member (without voting privileges). Honour them accordingly!

The informal constituency and/or advisory board

Not everyone can, or should, sit on your board or on a work group. Most people will state their willingness, when asked, to help in some way when the specific need arises. They also might consent to work on an advisory board. These people can be as helpful as those formally involved with your organization. Make sure they receive monthly updates on your organization by way of a bulletin or newsletter. Have an informal lunch with them two or three times a year. These "friends" often will tip you, for example, that a cabinet minister is looking for a certain type of proposal or that a new source of funds has been created. Also, an advisory board can consist of those prestigious names which are so effective when seeking corporate funding.

Community representation without policy control

Strictly speaking, an elected board of directors represents a cross section of the community views, while at the same time it is held responsible for how an organization conducts its affairs (Trusteeship).

However, many organizations seek a board of directors to:
- obtain credibility,
- carry out tasks with certain skills they possess.

These organizations do not want a community board to have final say over their policy direction. This situation is particularly true in arts organizations where a management-oriented board can stifle artistic growth.

The following diagram illustrates a method to obtain credibility and "task work" without surrendering policy control. When using this system an organization must ensure that all the organizational parts are informed in detail of all deliberations and activities of the other parts. This system of accountability gives an advisory board and patrons an opportunity to resign if they disagree with a board's decision, or to alert the board that the advisory board is moving in another direction.

An advisory board should possess voting powers and in every sense function like a board of directors with exceptions being made for certain issues. In essence the organization's legal board should retain the right of veto. All meetings must be open to all those participating at any organizational level.

```
┌─────────────────────────────────────┐
│                 Patrons             │
│  Prestige  persons  who  lend       │
│  their  names  to  an  organiza-    │
│  tion.  There  may  be  between     │
│  four and eight patrons.            │
└─────────────────────────────────────┘
┌─────────────────────────────┐
│       Board of Directors    │
│  Usually  a  founding  group│
│  which preserves a final veto on│
│  policy matters.            │
└─────────────────────────────┘

        ┌────────────────────────────────┐
        │                                │
        │                                │
        │            Advisory Board      │
        │  A group of workers and ad-    │
        │  visors.                       │
        │                                │
        │                                │
        └────────────────────────────────┘
```

Patron

According to the dictionary, a patron is a person who encourages and supports (financially or otherwise) a cause or endeavour. In practice, a patron is usually a prominent person (e.g., a member of Congress, a retired governor) who will endorse your goal and appear on your letterhead.

Further questions

You can always discuss your board's operating problems with other organizations. Why not have an annual get-together of community organization boards of directors and compare how they function.

Good Reading

Management and Fund Raising Centre, "Your Board of Directors," 1977. One of a series of how-to pamphlets, "Organizing Your Way to

44

Dollars.'' $1.50 each. Can be ordered from the Centre at 287 MacPherson Avenue, Toronto, Ontario M4V 1A4.

Guide for Board Organization in Social Agencies, published by Child Welfare League of America, Inc., 67 Irving Place, New York, New York 10003. A brochure covering:
- purpose of the board;
- board organization;
- bylaws;
- functional and ad hoc committees of the board;
- the executive director;
- channels of communication;
- evaluation of the agency's program and operations;
- bank accounts, bonding, financial accounting and insurance;
- board service and administrative volunteer manual.

So, You're on a Committee. New Jersey Community Training, Inc., 128 West State Street, Trenton, New Jersey 08608. A description of the work of committees and their role in overall governing board effectiveness. Includes points on the kinds of involvement required of committee members, the need for an agenda and a checklist guide to effective committee operation.

How to be an Effective Board Member. SEDFRE, 1 Penn Plaza, New York, New York 10001, 1973. A pamphlet on the "art" of board membership, describing what a good board is (differentiating between a working board and a rubberstamp board) and what a board does. There is a discussion about ad hoc and standing committees, planning and running meetings (with suggested ways of making meetings interesting), setting policy, public relations, evaluation and dealing with financial matters.

So, You Serve on a Board. Volunteer Bureau of Pasadena, Voluntary Action Center, 232 N. Lake Street, Pasadena, California 91101, 1972. A guide to board participation, discussing six broad areas:
• board functions;
• role of a board member;
• selection and term of membership;
• importance of training;
• board/staff responsibilities and relationship;
• evaluation.
The authors also describe practices leading to efficient conduct of meetings, points to consider in orientation and questions for evaluation.

Mrs. Charles Bolanz. "A Good Board Is a Victory." *New Thoughts on Board Function.* Chicago, Illinois: Child Care Association of Illinois, 1969.

Mary S. Rontzohn. *Better Board Meetings.* New York: Duotone Press, 1952.

The Seven Basic
Work Groups

*No snowflake in an avalanche
ever feels responsible.*
Unknown

The seven work groups

The following comprise the seven work groups within a well-run non-profit organizaton:

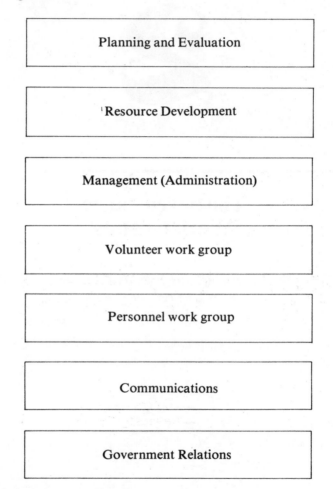

Planning and Evaluation

Resource Development

Management (Administration)

Volunteer work group

Personnel work group

Communications

Government Relations

In order to best use the information in this manual, your group should try to approximate this organizational model. Each group should then read the section that pertains to it and use the information fully during orientation and ongoing work. These work groups exist to support any program or project your organization undertakes. The people responsible for each program or project should list what they need from each work group and meet with a representative from each.

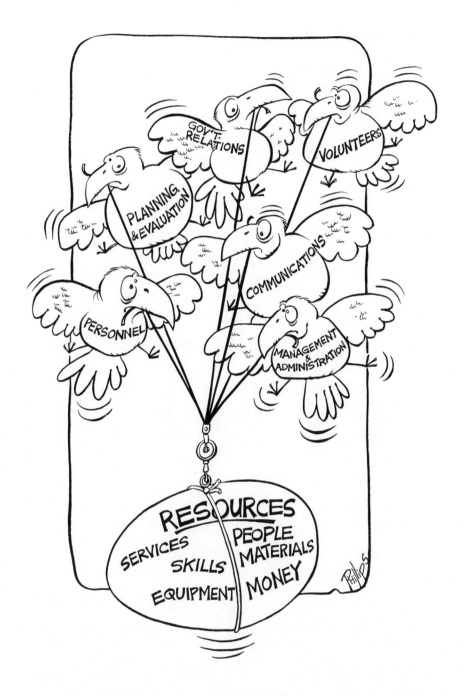

How the seven work groups function

MODEL A: with staff

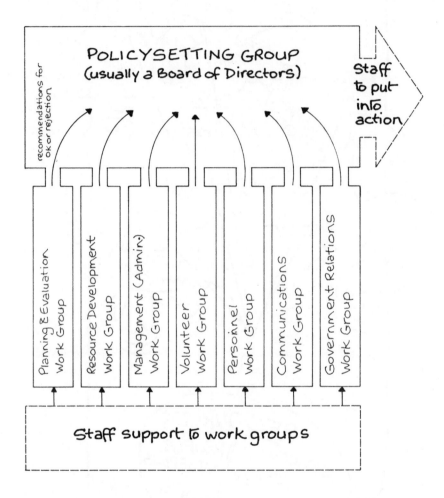

POLICYSETTING GROUP
(usually a Board of Directors)

recommendations for ok or rejection

Staff to put into action

Planning & Evaluation Work Group

Resource Development Work Group

Management (Admin.) Work Group

Volunteer Work Group

Personnel Work Group

Communications Work Group

Government Relations Work Group

Staff support to work groups

Notes:
1. Staff should be invited to assist each work group of the board. However, precautions must be taken not to undermine staff's primary implementation role with these planning functions.
2. The board and the work groups both monitor the progress of staff and programs, using the progress chart.

How the seven work groups function

MODEL B: *without staff*

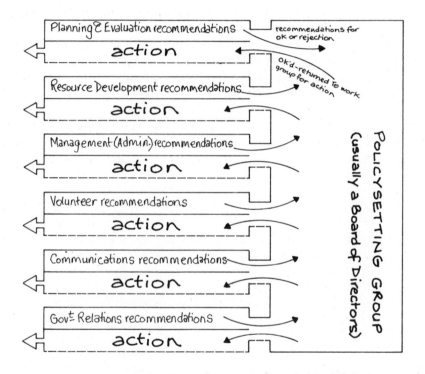

Notes:
1. Given the two-fold responsibility of the work groups, it is important not to overload them. Persons from outside your organization may bring special skills and talents to each work group.
2. Since there are no staff people, the personnel work group has been omitted from this model.

In general, these guidelines should be followed by the seven work groups:

1. It is important that *one* person only be a chairperson of a work group. It is equally important that this person, plus at least two others on each work group, are members of the policysetting group.

2. Each work group should either establish its own one-year schedule of activities and achievements, or have one formulated by the policysetting group. Either way, this schedule becomes the performance-measuring yardstick.

3. An eighth work group might be established to drawup a slate of new board members for year-end.

4. The management (administration) work group can also take on executive committee functions.

5

Planning and evaluation work group

A journey of a thousand miles starts under one's feet.

Lao Tsu

Responsibilities and priorities

This work group devises action to achieve the long and short range goals of the citizen group. It must also keep in touch with other similar citizen groups to avoid duplication of effort and to promote a sharing of essential program resources.

In newly established groups, priorities for programs are usually obvious. They are usually why a group of citizens has come together in the first place. It is generally the older, more established organization, which has taken on responsibilities over and above its original mandate, that begins to experience confusion. As the organization becomes increasingly visible over the years, demands are placed on it and saying "no" becomes a political rather than a straightforward decision.

Using techniques already discussed in this manual, a citizen group can fairly easily determine community needs and where the group

53

should place their program emphasis. A brainstorming session using any gathered information might be useful in determining the specific program needed.

I cannot believe that God
plays dice with the cosmos.
Albert Einstein

Program planning

The seven basic principles of program planning are:
1. Planners should keep the goals of the organization clearly before them as they work.
2. An effective program always develops out of the needs of those affected by it. (See "The Survey" and "The Research Study" in Chapter 3.)
3. Those who will carry out a program, and where possible, those affected by a program, must be able to contribute to its planning.
4. Planning ideas come from three sources: members of your group; its professional staff, if any; and outside people (including no. 3 above).
5. A readymade plan seldom can be adopted completely. Planning must take into account the individual differences of people, time and locale.
6. Planning should be fully recorded while being done. The record will help the evaluation and guide future planning for the program.
7. Program planning must include evaluation of both the plan and later the program after it has been in action for some time.

The key to successful programming

Once planners have determined the need for a program, the next step is to clarify the target groups — those for whom the program is designed. These questions must be asked:
• How can the purpose be made clear to the target group?
• What will interest target group?
• What does the target group need?
In the long run, the programs and projects of a citizen group are what attract people or turn them away. Citizens will only give their free time to activities with a clearly defined purpose and with which they are sympathetic.

People are attracted by:

- issues of direct concern to them, e.g., a polluted environment, care of the elderly, the need for a local theatre;
- meetings and conferences that lead to action, or give them information they need;
- activities that teach them skills, e.g., arts and crafts, study programs;
- activities that help them know their neighbours better.

Groups that can provide these experiences will be accepted as an important part of community life. When a series of programs leads by logical and visible steps to a particular achievement, the group will hold the interest of its citizen members.

The following are ways to get program ideas:

- brainstorming;
- opinion poll;
- suggestion box;
- informal conversation.

*If you're not very clever
you should be conciliatory.*
Benjamin Disraeli

Step-by-step program planning

1. Collect information about the need for a program.
2. Clearly decide on the intent or purpose of the program.
3. Plan how to put the program into action.
4. Map out the steps for achieving the program. (See "Chart Your Progress" in Chapter 7.)
5. Estimate the costs, in human, material and financial terms. Be realistic — e.g., budget on half your original estimated revenue, and increase estimated expenditures by 10 percent. Give a list of your resource needs to the resource development task group.
6. Evaluate the proposed plan. Are the long-range goals and immediate goals attainable?
7. Make advance arrangements. These include anything from submitting a brief for support to booking a community centre.
8. Make any needed requests to your other work groups, e.g., communications and resource development.
9. Prepare your schedule for the steps of putting the program into action. Responsibilities, confirmed in writing, should be given to individuals and a complete list displayed so everyone knows who's doing what.

10. Have an alternate plan — an idea of your options if the original plan has to be changed or cancelled.
11. Evaluate your program in action.

Good Reading

Program Planning for Community Leaders, No. 5. Ontario Ministry of Culture and Recreation, Sports and Fitness Division, Queen's Park, Toronto, Ontario.

Planning Better Programs — Leadership Pamphlet No. 2. Adult Education Association of the U.S., 1225-19th St. N.W., Washington D.C. 20036.

John C. DeBoer, *Let's Plan: A Guide to the Planning Process for Voluntary Organizations.* Philadelphia: United Church Press, 1970.

*It's easier to fight for one's
principles than to live up to them.*
Unknown

Program evaluation

Program evaluation keeps an organization on course and prevents it from flying blind. Evaluation is simply the process of finding honest and objective answers to such questions as:
• What are we doing?
• How well are we doing it?
• What are our group's attitudes and ideas?
• What are our programs and projects worth?
• What is the ability of our group to achieve our goals?
The judgments you make should be based on the evidence that comes from a systematic approach to the evaluation. Remember that good evaluation meets people on their own ground. It would be discouraging to apply the standards of London or Broadway stage to the productions of an amateur dramatic group on a local stage.

Who evaluates?

The best evaluation results when everyone measures progress. In this way, each person gains a deeper understanding and greater desire to improve, than if some higher or outside authority only carries out the

evaluation. However, in addition, a person who is not involved with your organization is useful in evaluation because he can see things more objectively. Make sure this person has experience in evaluating organizations. Questions this observer should ask are:

- Does the organization understand its purpose?
- Is the organization progressing toward its objectives? If not, why?
- Is the organization securing adequate resources and making the best possible use of them?
- Does the organization leadership encourage all participants to take increasing responsibility?

The observer's report must be objective and frank. It is not necessary to refer to people by name or criticize individuals. Your organization should take this report into account before making its final decisions. You may have to pay the observer an honorarium.

58

What is evaluated?

Questions are never indiscreet,
answers sometimes are.
Oscar Wilde

A community organization wants to evaluate two elements:
- how well its various systems, projects and programs work;
- the effect of the group on the problem or issue it deals with, and on the community as a whole;

Some organizational questions are:
- What proportion of members attend meetings regularly?
- How well do participants involve themselves in group activities and live up to their other responsibilities?
- Is the organization making good use of its resources and leadership?
- How effective are work groups or other committees?
- Has the behavior of the group's participants changed?
- Is there harmony in the group? If not, are there effective ways of dealing with the lack of harmony?
- How are staff-volunteer relations?
- Does your group have an appreciable effect on co-operation among other groups in your community?
- Is your group achieving its goals?

Evaluation techniques

These are many and varied. However, the simple technique of asking questions to the appropriate people and recording their replies will give you an idea of what is happening. Also, see "The Survey" and "The Research Study," in Chapter 3. There may be someone who can help you develop an in-depth questionnaire to evaluate your group and its impact in the community. Evaluation should take place each year. Don't be afraid to take drastic steps if needed.

Depend on the rabbit's foot if you will,
but remember, it didn't help the rabbit.
R.E. Shay

Good Reading

Evaluation: Notes for Community Leaders. Ontario Ministry of Culture and Recreation, Queen's Park, Toronto, Ontario.

Self-Evaluation Handbook for Voluntary Action Centers. National Center for Voluntary Action, 1785 Massachusetts Avenue, N.W., Washington, D.C. 20036, 1976.

Bobette W. Reigel. *Basic Feedback System: A Self-Assessment Process for Volunteer programs.* National Information Center on Volunteerism, P.O. Box 1807, Boulder, Colorado 80306, 1977.

6

Resource development work group

Whatever is not nailed down is mine.
What I can pry loose is not nailed down.
Collis P. Huntington

What is resource development?

Once your planning and evaluation work group has decided upon a goal and a plan to achieve it, your resource development work group should ask, "With what?"

Money is regarded by many as the single most important resource. It isn't! The most important resource is a group of committed people capable of using their various talents. And there are many other resources available.

To obtain these resources, you need to know:
1. Your shopping list — your group's total resource needs;
2. The types of donated resources available:
   - money,
   - people (volunteers, seconded or loaned staff or persons on sabbatical),
   - services and skills,
   - materials and equipment;
3. Who can provide these:
   - corporations, unions and professional associations,
   - government and government agencies,
   - foundations,

- educational institutions — public, secondary and post-secondary,
- community organizations,
- individuals.

4. How to obtain these resources;
5. How to use the resources efficiently and effectively;
6. How to report to donors on the way their donations are used.

The resource development work group should be an integral part of the budgeting process. This ensures that the various financial requirements of the organization's program are realistic.

The resource development work group will probably need to recruit influential outsiders to write letters to solicit support for the organization. The bulk of the resource development work group's activities should be organized in November/December with letters and representations hitting their targets in early January. The number of outsiders and the length of the campaign are determined by the size of your resource goals.

When meeting people who work for organizations that might donate resources, don't hesitate to ask them diplomatically about their organization's involvement with citizen groups, what donations they have made recently, and so forth. You'll know you have been successful when these people contact you with new information, becoming in effect your eyes and ears within their organization.

Some groups have programs deliberately opposed to the values and perhaps the existence of the institutions and organizations that normally can be relied upon to supply funds. These groups should select those sources of funds known to be sympathetic to their cause. It would be foolhardy to approach conventional sources of support — not to mention a waste of time.

Many resource donors would rather finance specific projects than ongoing operating expenses such as rent or basic staff salaries.

What you don't know won't help you
much either
Dan Bennett

Good Reading

Management and Fund Raising Centre, "Resource Development checklist," 1977. One of a series of how-to pamphlets, "Organizing Your Way to Dollars." $1.50 each. Can be ordered from the Centre at 287 MacPherson Avenue, Toronto, Ontario M4V 1A4.

Finding donors

Citizens organizations that are about to ask for donations are better equipped if they know about the activities and leanings of each potential donor. For this, it is crucial that your group is on the mailing lists of all potential resource donors, for:

- annual reports;
- monthly publications, e.g., newsletters, magazines;
- special bulletins or announcements;
- special publications, e.g., studies.

Make a list of all potential donors you intend to approach. The list should be divided up among your resource development group and each potential donor should be personally visited to make your first application. Once this face-to-face contact has been established, you are then in a position to write or phone for further requests. It is equally important to know which union or professional association is involved with each potential donor (if the donor is a company). They, too, should be contacted for donations purposes.(For more detailed information on securing funds, see "A Fund Raising Campaign" in this chapter.)

In addition, make sure you subscribe to local and national magazines and newspapers that are aimed at each of your potential donors, so you can understand their leanings. Some examples are:

For corporations: *Business Week, Forbes, Fortune, The Wall Street Journal, Dun's, Business and Society Review.*

For Unions: *American Labor, American Federationist, Monthly Labor Review.*

For communities: Local newspapers, neighbourhood newsletters, city and regional magazines.

For governments: *Congressional Digest, Federal Register, American Bar Association Journal.*

For colleges and universities: *American Association of University Professors Bulletin, American Association of University Women Journal, The Chronicle of Higher Education.*

Further information: *Ulrich's International Periodicals Directory,*

Ayers Newspaper and Periodicals Directory; or consult Bill Katz's *Magazines for Libraries* (New York: R.R. Bowker Company), an excellent directory that arranges periodicals by topic, provides circulations and other data, and gives a valuable analysis of each magazine's subject matter, editorial policies, and readership.

If you can afford it, hire the services of a clipping agency to clip all available articles about institutional giving to community groups. Your resource development group should examine this information once a month.

Corporations, businesses, unions and professional associations

*A businessman is a hybrid of a dancer
and a calculator.*
Paul Valery

In 1973, American corporations and businesses gave approximately $950 million to humanistic endeavors of all types. Though only a drop out of the brimming corporate bucket—profits before taxes in that year were $126.6 billion—these donations were still an important source of funds for nonprofit groups. Corporations also made substantial donations of products, equipment, services and skills.

How to find them
Standard and Poor's Register of Corporations, Directors and Executives lists corporations with officers and directors, followed by an alphabetical listing of executives, indicating the area of responsibility of each. Published by Standard and Poor, 345 Hudson Street, New York, New York 10014; available in large reference and all business libraries.

Other sources of information on corporations and their executives are:

Dun and Bradstreet Reference Book of Corporate Management. Dun and Bradstreet, Inc., 99 Church Street, New York, New York 10007. Biographies of officers and lists of directors of 2,400 U.S. corporations; 30,000 total listings.

Dun and Bradstreet Middle Market Directory. Lists 31,000 corporations with assets of $½ to $1 million.

Dun and Bradstreet Million Dollar Directory. 37,000 businesses worth $1 million or more. Both these directories list owners, officers and directors.

Thirty Thousand Leading U.S. Corporations. Year, Inc., 130 West 42nd Street, New York, New York 10036.

Directory of Directors in the City of New York. Directory of Directors Company, 350 Fifth Avenue, New York, New York 10001. Lists 15,000 executives and directors of 3,000 New York corporations.

F&S Index of Corporations and Industries. Predicasts, Inc., 11001 Cedar Avenue, Cleveland, Ohio 44106.

Aid to Education: Programs of Some Leading Business Concerns. Council for Financial Aid to Education, 680 Fifth Avenue, New York, New York 10017, 1976. Lists the executives responsible for philanthropy in many major corporations.

The Fortune Double 500 Directory. Fortune, Rockerfeller Center, New York, New York 10020. The 1,000 largest industrial concerns, with similar listings of the 50 largest banks, utilities, and transportation, insurance and retailing companies. This annual directory has the advantage of being easily obtained and cheap.

Virginia P. White, *Grants: How to Find Out About Them and What to Do Next.* New York: Plenum Press, 1975. A good general source of information about grants. Pages 159-169 discuss corporations.

Your local chamber of commerce can tell you about businesses in your area. In addition, unions and professional associations have become increasingly interested in supporting citizen groups. You can approach them for resources of all kinds. For information on unions, consult the *Directory of National Unions and Employee Associations*, published by the U.S. Government Printing Office.

What they have

Dollars: Corporations, including larger financial institutions, have donations budgets. Unions and professional associations usually have a central fund which they use for donations, and sometimes will canvass their membership for you.

People:
- volunteers
- members of a professional organization
- loaned employees
- staff on sabbatical
- staff on leave-of-absence

Services: Ask for the use of reproduction machinery; e.g., a photocopying machine. Ask for unused space for storage or office use. Ask for free transportation (air, rail, etc.).

Skills:	For example, ask:

Skills: For example, ask:
- an accounting firm to help with budget construction and everyday book keeping;
- a legal firm to handle your legal work;
- a promotion company to help organize a press conference;
- an advertising agency to plan an advertising campaign.

Equipment: Ask for office supplies, construction materials, spare furniture, etc. Approach an office equipment manufacturer for a typewriter or a desk, an automobile manufacturer for a truck . . . and so on.

Good Reading

Phillip I. Blumberg. *Corporate Responsibility in a Changing Society.* Boston: Boston University School of Law, 1972.

Neil W. Chamberlain. *The Limits of Corporate Responsibility.* New York: Basic Books, 1973.

Gideon Chagy. *The New Patrons of the Arts.* New York: Harry Abrams, Inc., 1972.

What corporations want to know

Man is an animal that makes bargains:
no other animal does this — no dog
exchanges bones with another.
Adam Smith

Following a random sampling, here's what corporations want to know about your group. Make sure that your presentation contains answers to the following questions. Other potential donors may want to know the same.

1. What is the age of your organization?
2. List the names of your board of directors.
3. How frequently does your board of directors meet?
4. How many paid employees do you have and how many volunteers participate?
5. How many people in the community did your services reach in the past year?
6. How many individuals, corporations, and government organizations supported your organization in the past year?

67

7. What is the purpose of your organization?
8. What are the accomplishments that your organization has realized in the past year? State the kinds of projects or activities you conducted.
9. What are the aims and objectives of your organization for the coming year?
10. Are you registered with the income tax department as a charitable nonprofit organization with income tax deductibility? If so, please state your registration number.
11. State your total operating income during the past year, your various sources of funds, your expenses and the difference between expenses and revenue.
12. State your financial plan for the coming year for the above items.
13. State your campaign objective and how much of this you expect to get from the business community.
14. Has your organization participated in any other campaigns in the past year, such as the United Way?
15. If a corporation makes a contribution to your organization, is there any potential for publicity or other forms of visibility in the community for having done so?
16. Are there any executives, directors, or employees of the potential donor corporation associated with or on the board of your organization?
17. How much would you expect to receive as a donation?
18. Are there any ways in which the potential donor could be of assistance to your organization other than a cash donation? Please specify.
19. Indicate the scope of your organization; that is, is it national, state, or local?
20. Is this campaign for capital funds or for operating expenses?
21. To what segment of the community are you directing your fund raising drive?
22. Is the fund raising campaign annual? If not, what period does it cover?

Government and government agencies

A likely impossibility is always preferable
to an unconvincing possibility.
Aristotle

Governments are usually large and complex. Make sure you know their structures, working procedures and personnel. Otherwise, you will overlook valuable resources. From all levels of government that affect your group, obtain a list of departments, their responsibilities and names of senior staff. Also ask for the names of all elected officials and what special responsibilities they have.

At one time the federal government did not go out of its way to explain its workings to the public; but since the passage in 1974 of a strengthened Freedom of Information Act, the problem for the curious citizen has been to avoid being overwhelmed in the avalanche of information his government is eager to make available to him. Major cities in every state have Federal Information Centers well-stocked with useful literature. Large public and university libraries have been designated as federal depositories, where extensive files of government documents are open to public scrutiny (see page 14).

Two invaluable publications are available at your library, or they may be ordered from the U.S. Government Printing Office, Washington, D.C. 20402. The *United States Government Manual* lists every federal agency, describes its organization and gives an account of its aims and activities. The *Catalog of Federal Domestic Assistance* lists all government aid programs. Federal assistance is not limited to grants of money: the *Catalog* indicates sources of aid in the form of equipment, goods, services and the use of facilities.

What they have

Dollars: There are three types of grants—
- *sustaining grants:* basic funding for ongoing operations, which may continue for a number of years
- *project grants:* limited to a specific time, for a specific purpose
- *contract or purchase of service:* by which a group agrees to carry out work for the government; e.g., public education, counselling, accommodation for needy persons, research

People:	• secondments (loans of paid staff) to work full or part time with your group. ACTION, a federal agency, provides paid staff to community organizations under a variety of programs. See page 132 for more information.
	• secondments from governments in other parts of the U.S.
	• volunteers from government employee associations or unions
	• sabbatical leaves for employees to work within your group (partly or wholly financed by the government)
	• sabbatical leave for government workers from overseas to work for six to nine months with your group. (First check with the State Department to find out about working visas. They may also know of organizations in other countries who wish to place people in the United States, or when this has been done previously.)
Services:	• research and survey services, particularly statistics
	• general duplication and printing services
	• consulting and information on every subject you could imagine
	• program, meeting and conference space
Equipment:	• loans or donations of office equipment
	• loans of film, photography, or video equipment
	• donations of office supplies, and so forth

Educational institutions (primary and secondary schools, universities, community colleges, and technical colleges)

Look in your telephone book for local boards of education. Contact your state's department of education for lists of colleges, etc.

Monitor *all* (including sub-committee) trustees' meetings. Make a point of being on all school board mailing lists. Know their organizational structure and the names of senior staff.

These institutions will often welcome your request for resources, because they want to work more closely with the community. They are concerned about becoming too isolated — remind them of this.

What they have

Dollars: It is most unusual for educational systems to donate funds to nonprofit organizations unless they are collaborating on a project.

People: A large student body can be mobilized to:
- help in fund raising projects, ranging from car washes to door-to-door solicitation;
- obtain community-wide support for an issue;

Individual students can be approached to act as volunteers at all levels of a community group. They also can be loaned to a project as part of their term work; e.g., to design a lobby process, to work with a disabled person, to do a survey, to help organize your resource development work group, and so forth. This arrangement is often referred to as a field placement or practicum. In order to gain this assistance, you must emphasize the educational return to the student.

Teachers and professors can be recruited as volunteers. They also can spend extensive periods (six to nine months) working with your group as part of a sabbatical. Choose the department most involved with your area of concern and contact teaching staff.

Services: A full range of services usually is available, including:
- meeting and conference rooms and related services;
- office space;
- access to computers for information searches;
- community research services;
- use of printing and duplicating machinery;
- design and layout for brochures, etc.

Skills: Individual students and teachers have most skills needed by a community group, including:
- management or administrative abilities;
- skills peculiar to your projects;
- techniques for writing and presenting briefs.

Equipment:
- use of video equipment, film projectors, etc.;
- office and art supplies;
- spare office equipment.

71

Foundations

The 30,000 privately endowed foundations in the U.S. disburse more than $2 billion a year. Foundations range in size from such giants as the Ford Foundation, which gives away about $200 million annually, to the very small entities with assets of a few thousand dollars. The big, well-known foundations tend to receive far more than their proportionate share of grant applications, with the result that the great majority of these applications are turned down. A modest group with modest needs might do well to look into the grant programs offered by small and middle-sized foundations.

A good place to begin is with the *Annual Register of Grant Support*, published by Marquis Who's Who, 4300 W. 62nd St., Indianapolis, Indiana 46206, and available at larger libraries. This reference describes the programs of *all* grant-giving institutions, private and public. Organized by disciplines—humanities, social sciences, environmental studies and so forth—the *Annual Register* provides a useful overview of grants available in your area of interest.

The richest and most reliable sources of information about foundations are the three national and sixty regional reference collections of the Foundation Center. The national collections are located at:

The Foundation Center
888 Seventh Avenue
New York, New York 10019

The Foundation Center
1001 Connecticut Avenue N.W.
Washington, D.C. 20036

Donors' Forum
208 South La Salle Street
Chicago, Illinois 60604

The regional collections are located in public and university libraries in major cities. In addition to a wealth of other material, all collections include *The Foundation Directory,* also available through Columbia University Press, 136 South Broadway, Irvington-on-Hudson, New York 10533. This is the definitive reference on foundations.

Good Reading
F. Emerson Andrews. *Foundation Watcher*. Lancaster, Pa.: Franklin and Marshall College, 1973.

Merrimon Cuninggim. *Private Money and Public Service: The Role of Foundations in American Society*. New York: McGraw-Hill Book Company, 1972.

City or municipal foundations
Some communities ease the strain on municipal budgets by setting up their own foundations, to which citizens can contribute as to a charity. Many of the 240 community foundations in the U.S. have given important support to experimental projects and community action groups. The New York Community Trust, the largest institution of this kind, disburses about $10 million annually. Other important municipal foundations are the Chicago Community Trust, the Cleveland Foundation, the San Francisco Foundation, and the Permanent Charity Fund of Boston.

Good Reading
Jack Shakely. "Community Foundations." *The Grantsmanship Center News*, 1015 West Olympic Boulevard, Los Angeles, California 90015, 1976.

Community organizations

These are vitally important to your group. They include:
- volunteer centres;
- information centres;
- libraries;
- service clubs
- religious organizations;
- United Way;
- other community groups (citizen groups, social service organizations, etc.).

Volunteer Centres
As the name suggests, these recruit volunteers for all community organizations. They will take your specifications and seek volunteers to fit them. Look in your phone book, call your library, or contact your local Voluntary Action Center—if you have one. If not, then get in touch with:

73

National Center for Voluntary Action
1785 Massachusetts Avenue N.W.
Washington, D.C. 20036
(telephone: 202-797-7800)

Ask for a copy of the *Technical Services Guide*, a list of services and publications available from the NCVA.

Information centres and libraries

Community information centres and public libraries can provide space for meetings, bulletin and display boards, audio-visual and other equipment, resource people—and information. Libraries, as one of the few public institutions open to people of all ages and interests, have in recent years become important centres of community and neighbourhood organization.

Service clubs

> *The first Rotarian was the first*
> *man to call John the Baptist Jack.*
> H.L. Mencken

Examples of service clubs are the Kiwanis, Rotary, Junior League, and Lions.

Most service clubs are quite conservative. Citizen rights and pressure groups of all types may have difficulty getting the support of a service club. However, nothing ventured, nothing gained!

Present your request for special project support in April or May, for the next fall. Most clubs are inactive during the summer.

What they have

Dollars: The amount varies from $25 to $2,000 and up for community programs.

People: Service clubs are an excellent source of "helping" volunteers. Some are highly trained for voluntary work; e.g., the Junior League.

Services: Fund raising events can seriously drain the energies of your group. Service clubs enjoy holding these events and have experience running them. You can ask a club to organize an event for you.

74

Equipment: Since most of these can be reached via club membership, you should present your "shopping list" of what you need (preferably at the end of a speech about your group's work).

Religious organizations

What they have
Dollars:
- Larger denominations have national head offices which give funds to community projects that square with their national community service priorities.
- Most denominations are members of the World Council of Churches in Geneva, which has funds for projects with international implications operating in the U.S.

People:
- In many communities, religious organizations are still the best source of volunteers. Local churches can ask their head office for priests and ministers in training, to be placed in a community with a special project. Try them for yours!
- To obtain broad-based support for a project, approach an ecumenical council (a co-ordinating group made up of all churches in the community).

Services:
- Religious organizations may, although rarely, be prepared to launch a fund raising drive or special event for your group.
- use of duplicating and general office machinery
- meeting and conference space
- publicity (via sermons, church magazine, and so forth)
- temporary use of office space for your project
- community organization (sometimes)

Equipment:
- office furniture, etc.
- congregations can be approached with your "shopping list."

The United Way
(Previously known as Red Feather, Community Chest and United Appeal)

The United Way is a major supplier of dollars to community organizations.

75

For many nonprofit organizations, the United Way is the most important source of operating funds, which often are difficult to obtain from other sources. The United Way provides relative security for operating funds from year to year, and thus gives a group the invaluable opportunity to develop long-range planning.

United Way objectives are:

- to save time and money (more than 90¢ of each dollar is distributed to participating organizations), and to lessen the number of separate campaigns.
- to co-ordinate the distribution of funds, and balance social services in the community.
- to test the need for new services. And if a long-term need is proven by a service, to hand it over to government for financing.

Your group must be registered as a charitable organization under the IRS code (see Chapter 4).

Once a member of United Way, you cannot publicly solicit funds from other community sources (the general public, businesses or corporations). However, you can:

- charge a fee for your service;
- charge membership fees;
- approach government and foundations;
- solicit bequests;
- privately solicit a select number of individuals.

Before you approach United Way for membership, check:

- whether you can live with their public fund raising restrictions;
- their priority rating for your type of group;
- any other demands (acceptance of bi-yearly evaluations, etc.).

Given the slowed-down growth of United Way, it is unusual to obtain more than an average increase of 3 to 5 percent annually. Thus, it is important to secure a reasonable level of support at your time of entry.

In some people's view, the United Way is controlled by rich corporations who give only token dollars for "bandaid" solutions to community problems. It may be true that the massively orchestrated advertising and publicity that characterize United Way fund drives do tend to overshadow—and draw money away from—smaller and more innovative groups.

The address of the national office of the United Way is:

United Way of America
801 North Fairfax Street
Alexandria, Virginia 22313.

How to secure resources

The pessimist spends all his time worrying
about how he can keep the wolf from the door.

The optimist refuses to see the wolf until
he seizes the seat of his pants.

The opportunist invites the wolf in and
appears the next day in a fur coat.

Unknown

This section outlines the best ways to secure
- dollars,
- services,
- skills,
- materials,
- equipment.

Recruiting people (volunteers) is discussed in Chapter 8, "The Volunteer Work Group."

Be brave! Don't go cap in hand, but proudly, with dignity. You must feel that you are doing something useful — if not don't do it. Don't be overly aggressive, but believe in yourselves and your group.

Your resource development work group should keep a log of:
- whom you approach each year;
- what you get;
- when the fiscal year of each donor and potential donor begins, and thus when is the best time to make a submission to them.

How to secure dollars

If at first you don't succeed,
you're doing about average.

Leonard Louis Levinson

A brief with a covering letter signed by a prominent citizen presented in person is the most effective way of soliciting funds.

Many corporations still are not able to properly evaluate requests for funds from nonprofit groups. Thus, they feel more secure about requests when the names of their peers or colleagues appear on your letterhead. If these people do not fit into your board of directors, recruit them for your resource development work group or as an advisory body to it. But make sure the names are visible on your fund raising material.

People and organizations who donate funds and other resources usually support causes, programs, projects or new facilities,
- *not* institutions because of their name,
- *not* operating expenses, and especially
- *not* operating deficits!

Giving is prompted by the emotions and then rationalized. You will be the most successful if your project contains some appeal to the emotions, supported, of course, by a logical framework.

For corporations and financial institutions, submit a brief to the head person or the donations committee (to the senior person at union headquarters). Remember, they want in-depth material but often don't look at it. Write a good synopsis of your brief and use it as the basis of your covering letter. Submit your brief the month before their new fiscal year begins, so you can be "first in the door" when the allocation of funds is being decided.

Whenever possible, get the support of other individuals or organizations for your submission. Have them write letters directly to the source of funds or include such letters with your brief.

The ideal is to present the brief in person, then send a followup letter highlighting your presentation. However, this is costly and time-consuming. The law of diminishing returns dictates that you must do this with care and with some idea of how good your chances are. *The larger the number of contacts you make, the lower the return per contact and the higher the fund raising costs! Don't spread yourselves too thin!*

To some extent, this caution is not needed with a widespread mailing campaign. However, remember that at least a phone followup is better than none at all!

An informal phone call often will set the wheels in motion for people, products, services, skills and materials. It takes a longer, more formal process to secure dollars.

Good Reading

Harold James Seymour. *Designs for Fund Raising; Principles, Patterns and Techniques.* New York: McGraw-Hill Book Company, 1966.

Howard R. Mirkin. *The Complete Fund Raising Guide.* New York: The Public Service Materials Center, 1975. This book includes sections on:

- why raise money;
- matching funds;
- identifying your group to the community;
- educating the public about a problem;
- encouraging new membership;
- creating reserves;
- how to obtain support through membership;
- government grants;
- fund raising through direct mail;
- conducting a capital funds campaign;
- special events;
- organizing campaign publicity;
- professional fund raising managers;
- raising funds from business and labour.

The Bread Game. Glide Publications, 330 Ellis Street, San Francisco, California 94102, $1.95 postpaid. An 88-page handbook exploring "the realities of foundation fund raising."

Fund Raising Management. Hoke Communications, 224 Seventh Street, Garden City, Long Island, New York 11530. A bi-monthly magazine featuring ideas about fund raising and examples of successful techniques.

Scott M. Cutlip. *Fund Raising in the United States.* New Brunswick, New Jersey: Rutgers University Press, 1965.

Irving R. Warner. *The Art of Fund Raising.* New York: Harper and Row. A manual for novice fund raisers.

Joseph Dermer. *How to Write Successful Foundation Presentations.* New York: The Public Service Materials Center, 1972. Includes:
- how to write your presentation, with step-by-step examples;
- how to cultivate foundations;
- how to get appointments;
- how to improve your chances while your proposal is being considered.

Fund raising letters

These have become a science unto themselves. They are important either as a covering letter for a brief or by themselves as a followup.

State the problem, what is being done, what needs to be done, what your group proposes to do, and how. (See "How to Write a Brief," starting on page 92.) Make a direct request, and suggest dollar amounts. Illustrate what $10 will do, how $25 will be used, etc. Show a believable and reachable goal.

Donors may not care much about your organization, but they do care about the people you help. Tell the story of one person who is receiving help from your program, and include a photograph if possible. Translate your material needs into human terms.

Write in the style you use in speaking. The words you use should be warm and personal (I, we, you, your, etc.) instead of stiff and pompous. Use action words ("we are doing") instead of passive words ("it is being done"). Use short sentences and short paragraphs (three or four sentences), but your letter need not be short — you don't want the reader to finish reading it before he has decided to give a donation.

See also "Direct Mail Campaign" on page 107.

Good Reading

Management and Fund Raising Centre, "Fund Raising Letters," 1977. One of a how-to pamphlet series, "Organizing Your Way to Dollars." $1.50 each. Can be ordered from the Centre at 287 MacPherson Avenue, Toronto, Ontario M4V 1A4.

Joseph Dermer, ed. *America's Most Successful Fund Raising Letters.* New York: The Public Service Materials Center. This book gives examples of fund raising letters, with commentaries by their authors, from a wide range of nonprofit groups.

How to secure services, skills, materials and equipment

> *Nothing is so often irretrievably missed*
> *as a daily opportunity.*
> Ebner-Eschenbach

Community groups should let themselves dream, "What should we have if we are to do the best job possible?" State your idea in a *shopping list.* Against each item, place the names of manufacturers, community groups, individuals, etc., who may be able to donate or loan that item.

Using an informal telephone approach, explain to each potential donor who you are and what your group is doing. Say your request is for services, etc., instead of dollars, as part of your resource development program. Ask for the needed item and also ask if there is an application process.

Make presentations to organizations or local community groups to prompt their members into a non-monetary loan or donation. Present your shopping list to as many likely donors as possible.

Once each year, ask your local newspaper to publish a list of resources your group needs. If the newspaper will not donate the space, ask them by way of the advertising department to seek out sponsors for the space.

Don't settle for less than a quarter of a page. The sponsor's name can appear at the bottom of the advertisement.

Planning a fund raising campaign

The following is a step-by-step outline to launching a fund raising campaign. Like all other sections in this book, it must be adapted to fit your particular needs.

In addition to following the steps outlined here, a planning group should use all available references and plan in detail a blueprint for each section of the campaign organization.

Good luck!

Steps	*Comments*
1. Contact other similar organizations to see how they planned their fund raising campaigns and what results they achieved. Travel to other parts of the country if necessary.	Most important — don't skimp on this step.
2. Develop a question and answer sheet covering all aspects of your organization with a special emphasis on the exact need for the fund raising campaign.	This is the best way of building your case to convince and recruit your campaign chairman recruitment committee. This information can also be used to develop your main campaign brochure.
3. Refine question and answer sheet by testing it on known sympathetic and unsympathetic outsiders.	Don't skip this process. We're all too close to our own situations to see the wood from the trees.
4. Develop an impressive campaign brochure. Pay a	From the very beginning you need to convince people that your

81

professional if necessary. Make certain that illustrations and diagrams are used whenever possible.

cause is important. A professionally written brochure will present the case more clearly than anything else.

5. Form a communications committee consisting of persons who work in or know the communications field. They are responsible for your opening press conference, resulting follow-up, speakers bureau to speak with all local organizations and keeping the media in ongoing touch with your campaign's progress.

This communications work creates the all-important "environment" in which to conduct your campaign.

6. Obtain at least one feature newspaper story before you start your search for a campaign chairman.

Use this feature as a credibility getting device to convince persons to join your campaign chairman recruitment committee.

7. Organize a campaign chairman recruitment committee. This committee should consist of approximately six persons who are known to have friends who are senior in the business community. Their job is only to find a campaign chairman.

8. Recruit a campaign chairman.

Choose someone who is known to have economic leverage, is widely respected and preferably has volunteer fund raising campaign experience.

9. Campaign chairman selects a campaign executive.

The executive consists of four to six persons. Their job is to organize the campaign divisions and help the campaign chairman secure a chairman for each division.

10. The chairman and his executive must determine that the campaign goal is realistic and then set deadlines, budgets, etc.

11. Set up campaign headquarters and organize all administration systems including recording all donations, receipt procedures, etc. Also establish budgets.

This is a straightforward matter, yet vital to the success of your campaign. Attempt to locate all campaign functions in the corporate building where your campaign chairman works. This is functionally more effective and gives your campaign a recognized prestige. You should not spend more than 15 percent of your private fund raising goal on the costs of fund raising.

12. Organize campaign divisions. These ideally are:
- Financial institutions
- Trust companies
- Oil and gas companies
- Insurance companies
- Foundations
- Merchandising outlets
- Communications industry
- Construction, real estate, developers
- Distilleries and breweries
- Forest products
- Automotive industry
- Major mining and chemical companies
- Food processing and tobacco companies
- Metal fabricators and steel companies
- Pharmaceuticals
- Electronics and electrical appliances
- Transport, utilities and pipelines

- Industrials (under $25 million annual gross)
- Major industrials (over $25 million annual gross)
- Business equipment and machinery
- Professionals and associations
- Prominent individuals

13. Recruit campaign personnel including:
    - Divison chairmen
    - Canvassers for each division including executives

All division chairmen should be senior persons who possess leverage with their division prospects (potential donors). These can be amended to fit your local situation.

14. Print letterhead with your organization's board members' names prominently displayed on the left hand side and your campaign division chairmen on the right hand side.

Unfortunately, regardless of how good your project is, it usually receives support only because of who is involved with it.

15. Meet separately with division chairmen to ensure that *all* prospects are listed in their division and to set a goal for each prospect and hence each division.

Once a master list is established for each division, make up cards that can be taken away and used by each canvasser. A canvasser should not be responsible for more than ten cards each.

16. Meet collectively and individually with division chairmen to give them orientation and canvassing materials. Set deadlines.

The canvassing options available to a division chairman are:
1. to convene a series of luncheons with a senior person from each prospect;
2. either the division chairman (if he's senior enough) or someone else well known to the business community to write a letter to each prospect requesting support and introducing a key volunteer or staff person who will call and canvass personally.

17. Secure bell ringer (first) donations from those known to be sympathetic to your campaign. These donations must be substantial!

In order to secure these large bell ringer donations, encourage a pledge arrangement over a three- to five-year period. Use the pledge system throughout your campaign. Press release the bell ringer donations.

18. Request that your mayor or governor write a letter to all those you are about to approach for funds.

This costs you nothing and will open a hundred doors!

19. Convene a media conference to announce a first-phase campaign to the media with accompanying list of your early donations.

A first-phase announcement permits you to canvass prospects a second time (second phase) without it being construed that your campaign is failing. This allows firms to fit you into a new fiscal budget or simply reconsider. Allow at least 6 months for your first-phase campaign.

20. Continue media campaign with usual weekly releases, feature stories, etc.

This ongoing media coverage is vital if you are to obtain a broad base of community support and create a sympathetic environment for your fund raising campaign.

21. Commence canvassing of all prospects.

There are no quick answers! Always attempt to see in person each prospect — a letter will only open the door.

22. Convene a weekly breakfast reporting meeting to include all division chairmen. Preview achievements, review deadlines, etc.

This gives the campaigners a sense of identity, peer competition and support for one another and other benefits. The breakfast time usually ensures a short meeting and takes a minimum of volunteers' business time.

23. Commence phase two of the pledge campaign.

This is a recanvass of some prospects who have given nothing or a nominal sum. Their earlier response is *not* brought into contention, rather an attempt is made to see if they will pledge an amount for the years ahead. It enables them to be associated with your project at a time when it is convenient for them.

24. A very special thank you ceremony for all the volunteers who worked with you.

Organizations take too much for granted. Always treat your campaign workers with recognition and gratitude, particularly at the end of a long grind. Think of something special.

The New Theatre
Open Circle Theatre
Le Théâtre du P'tit Bonheur

Adelaide Court/Cour Adélaïde
57 Adelaide Street East
Toronto, Ontario
M5C 1K6
(416) 363-1031

Under the distinguished patronage of/
Sous le patronage distingué de:

The Honourable William G. Davis, Q.C.,
   Premier of Ontario
The Honourable W. Z. Estey,
   Chief Justice of Ontario
The Honourable John Roberts,
   Secretary of State
The Honourable Gregory T. Evans,
   Chief Justice of the High Court of Ontario
The Honourable R. Roy McMurtry, Q.C.,
   Attorney-General for Ontario
Paul Godfrey, Metropolitan Toronto Chairman
David Crombie, Mayor of Toronto
The Honourable G. A. Gale, Q.C., L.L.D.
His Honour Chief Judge W. E. C. Colter
His Honour Chief Judge Frederick C. Hayes

Advisory Board/Comité consultatif:

   Campaign Chairman,
     Burnett M. Thall
   Campaign Vice-Chairman,
     Jane Drynan

* Harry W. Arthurs
   J. Perry Borden
   Mrs. Gerald D. Brown
* George A. Cohon
   Joanne Cooper
* William A. Dimma
* William I. K. Drynan
   Beatrice Fischer
   John Fisher
   Elsa Franklin
* Dean M. L. Friedland, Q.C.
   Pierre Genest, Q.C.
* Dr. Reva Gerstein
   Philip B. Gurvich
   Helen Hutchinson
   William Kilbourn
   Victor Koby
* The Honourable Donald S. Macdonald
   Sanford McFarlane, C.A.
   James H. McLaughlin, Q.C.
* Jean P. W. Ostiguy
   Tom Patterson, O.C.
   Lexie Roberts
   Allan C. Rose, Q.C.
   Donald V. Stirling
   Edward G. Turner
   Etienne Wermester

* Honorary/Honoraire

PATRONS

ADVISORY BOARD

SLOGAN

- a long-awaited venture in theatre, restoration and common sense -

a registered charitable organization supported by voluntary contributions/une organisation charitable dûment enregistrée, subsistant de contributions bénévoles

Sample letterhead

87

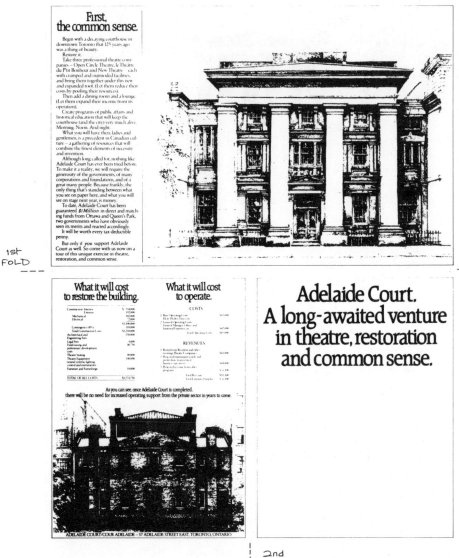

1st
FOLD

2nd
FOLD

Sample fund raising brochure

Next, the restoration.

The building you just left the front of was designed in 1852, by Frederick Cumberland, a prominent architect, who with William Storm also designed St. James Cathedral (just down the street), University College, and the major renovations to Osgoode Hall.

Cumberland's and Storm's buildings were drawn to last.

This one served as York County Courthouse from 1852 to 1900, then as the Municipal Hall, for York County and finally as a Police Magistrate's Court.

A Hall? A Court?…

Why of course!

A theatre is not much different in shape really, and besides, this court is blessed with a huge council chamber above the actual courtroom.

Which means that Adelaide Court will contain two performing spaces in addition to common administrative, rehearsal and workshop space for the three companies.

THE ADELAIDE THEATRE
will hold 281 people with portable seating and stage layouts.

THE COURT THEATRE
will be a 150-seat theatre by night, and a mock courtroom by day (more on this later).

Stop for a moment now and look carefully at the side-view interior drawing below.

Notice the elegant spiral staircase on the right.

It will be preserved, as will the original interiors of both theatre spaces.

In fact, by working closely with the Toronto Historical Board and the Ontario Heritage Foundation, we shall do our utmost to see that the Courthouse is restored to its original splendour.

Now look at the people having their dinner in the lower-level restaurant.

You might ask yourself what a nice restaurant is doing in a place like this.

Well, for one, it (and the 73-seat lounge upstairs) will be providing at least $44,000 (and likely $88,000) in additional revenues to support the three theatre groups. For

Restaurant and Lounge

another, they will introduce thousands of non-theatre goers to a theatre atmosphere, and provide an exciting meeting place for people in the performing arts.

Above the restaurant, you can see two levels of foyer space for patrons of the two theatres, and at the very top of the theatres, and at the very top of the building, a sophisticated lighting control room.

Because this is only a side-view drawing, you can't see through to the office space for the three theatre companies, (one on each floor), or the lounge and rehearsal space.

But do not worry; they will be here on opening day – January 1, 1978.

Finally the theatre.

Because Adelaide Court is a public building, restored largely with public money, it has an obligation to serve the widest possible cross-section of the community that gave it new life.

Thus, Adelaide Court will mean more than just theatre alone.

It will also mean:

"Issues on Trial", a courtroom drama series held at lunchtime, where the beliefs of well-known men and women will be placed on trial. Real-life lawyers will act as judge, prosecution and defense, while an audience of 150 will act as jury.

The trials will all take place in the Court Theatre using original courtroom fittings. It is expected that "Issues on Trial" will broadcast live on television.

We also mean that students from all over Ontario will be able to use the courtroom by re-creating actual cases from the

1850's, and in the process, learn first hand much about Canadian history, common law and theatrical improvisation.

The bottom lines.

Much of the common sense about Adelaide Court is in the numbers.

In all, we expect 150,000 to 180,000 people to visit us every year – attending the theatre productions, participating in the public affairs and student education programs, and using the lounge and restaurant.

The savings make even more sense.

Adelaide Court will give three important theatre companies a much-needed, magnificent new home – at no more cost than their present facilities.

This little miracle will occur because Adelaide Court lets them cut their costs by sharing them.

And boost their income by generating money to support theatre programs.

In addition, it will provide a much-needed home for French-speaking theatre in English-speaking Canada.

But what makes the most sense of all about Adelaide Court is what it can do for the planning of Canada's other cultural enterprises.

Student Education Program

As one very practical man was moved to suggest: it is the ultimate in organizational creativity and pragmatism.

And in these harsh times, ladies and gentlemen, those big words are what survival is all about.

The tour is over.

But the work has just begun.

We hope that you will help us, and we believe that you will want to.

And with $1 million already secured, our campaign goal from the private sector is $574,750.

So thank you, and au revoir.

The three theatre groups.

Open Circle Theatre.
— Founded in 1972, Open Circle provides entertainment with a strong social consciousness. Last season's four plays were produced on a total budget of $120,000 to an audience of 8,000 people, up 2,000 from the previous season. Open Circle is directed by Sylvia Tucker and Ray Whelan. It plays in any available space.

Le Théâtre du P'tit Bonheur.
— As the only French-language theatre, T.P.B. reflects the francophone culture through

its productions and workshops. Almost half its audience is English-speaking.

Last season, T.P.B. staged five plays (for $90,000) on the third floor of a building in the Broadview and Danforth area, where the workshop doubled as a dressing room. Ten thousand people saw the plays, more than double T.P.B.'s audience of three years ago.

New Theatre.
Founded in 1973, by Jonathan Stanley, New Theatre presents plays that are new to Canada. Located in the Bathurst Street United Church, it

has enjoyed the largest growth of all Toronto's professional alternate theatres. From 1975 to 1976, its audience increased 119% over three productions. New Theatre's budget last year was $120,000.

All three theatres are non-profit organizations supported by operating grants from the City of Toronto, Metropolitan Toronto, The Ontario Arts Council and The Canada Council.

Each theatre also provides services outside its regular season. For example, they mount workshops to develop new plays, artists and technicians, and participate in many other cultural projects throughout the Metro Toronto area.

1st
FOLD

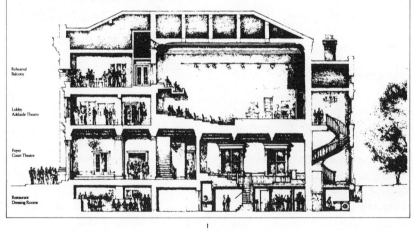

Rehearsal
Balcony

Lobby
Adelaide Theatre

Foyer
Court Theatre

Restaurant
Dressing Rooms

2nd
FOLD

Approximate campaign budget for campaign between $500,000 and $1 million goal

PROJECTED CAMPAIGN BUDGET, 1-YEAR DURATION AS STRUCK IN 1977

Personnel (fees, wages, etc.)

Campaign director	$12,000	
— bonus of 2% for every $100,000 raised from the private sector, or proportion thereof	10,000	
Secretary assistant (salary & benefits)	10,000	
Part-time typist	1,500	
Part-time bookkeeper	1,000	
		$34,500

Public Information and Promotion

Pamphlets and leaflets	$ 3,500	
Photography and blowups for display	2,500	
Special events (cocktail party series)	3,000	
Public relations personnel (fees)	4,000	
		$13,000

Rent	$ 4,000	
Furniture	1,000	
		$ 5,000

General Expenses

Cards and forms	$ 1,000	
Letterheads and envelopes	1,500	
Office supplies	1,500	
Reference materials	250	
Postage	1,000	
Duplicating	500	
Telephone	600	
Transportation and delivery	250	
Entertainment	200	
Audit and insurance	300	
Contingency	2,000	
		$ 9,100

GRAND TOTAL		$61,600

Note: Many of these items may be eliminated or substantially reduced as charges against the campaign budget if arrangements are made for loaned personnel and donated or at-cost services and supplies, and if volunteer assignments are carried out according to schedule.

More tips on fund raising

- If at all possible, show how your project will make an impact at a national or regional level. This will secure you more funds than just a local community project.
- Emphasize on *all* your literature that donations are tax deductible.
- Always develop a pledge card. Always accept a larger donation over two or three years rather than a modest one in the year of the canvass.
- Wherever possible, try to establish giving levels, for example:
  Corporations and Foundations

Friends of (the name of your project)	$500 or more
Benefactors for donations of	$1,000 or more
Patrons for donations of	$10,000 or more
Grand Patrons for donations of	$25,000 or more

  The same giving categories should apply to individuals only halved in amount, with the addition of sustaining membership at $100 or less.
- Most campaigns will require a small yet competent staff. Usually a secretary, part-time bookkeeper and a campaign director. Sometimes it is possible to obtain the services of a loaned executive whose time is donated to the campaign part- or full-time by a corporation. A fund raising firm will sometimes provide staffing as part of their fee.
- Often foundations are interested in a specific part of your project. Check this out in advance of your approach and if necessary, write a brief explaining in detail their area of interest.
- Public funds from governments often represent the larger portion of funds required for a project. Since these funds are sometimes secured from different levels of government, it is wise to convene a meeting of *all* appropriate officials before you commence your fund raising campaign. As them for suggestions regarding your project's design, etc. and then ask if they think they will be able to support it.

91

Good Reading

Bibliography of Fund Raising and Philanthropy. National Catholic Development Conference, 130 East 40th Street, New York, New York 10016. A valuable reference listing more than 1,000 books and periodicals about fund raising published through March, 1975. Annual supplements are available.

How to write a brief

*All the world's a stage and most of us
are desperately un-rehearsed.*
Sean O'Casey

Many groups will not need a brief as detailed as that described here. Use your own judgment; apply this information to suit your group's needs.

The written brief is the most accepted way of asking for a donation of resources. It must be clear and concise. Your brief represents your understanding of the problem or issue, and your ability to accomplish your goal.

While formats vary, here are the essentials, in the order they should appear in your brief. Each section should be no longer than a page. Short briefs can be just as effective as long ones. To write a short brief, use the headings described here, but only write sentences under each.

1. Title
Give your project a title, one which accurately and concisely describes it's intent. Beware of "cute" acronyms (DEATH — Developing Everyone's Approach to Happiness, Inc., or RAPE — "Regional Association for the Protection of the Environment"), they can discredit your efforts.

2. Table of contents
On the first page inside the cover, list by page number each section and sub-section of your brief, including your synopsis and appendices.

3. Synopsis

For the busy reader, this is the most important section of your brief. Describe in sequence, briefly, each section of the brief. Use, at the most, between 60 and 90 words per section.

4. Introduction

The general background on which your project is based — an overview of the general social, religious, cultural, scientific or organizational context into which your project fits.

5. Statement of need

Describe the overall condition that your project is directed at. Give proof (quote studies, if available, etc.) that the condition exists and why it is important to change it.

6. Statement of purpose

State generally what *you* are going to do to change the condition. Then state why. List your long- and short-term goals for the project.

7. Theoretical framework

Outline your assumptions about the methods your project will use. State how they will be effective. For a demonstration project, state how it will differ from what has been done elsewhere. Also, state what impact it will have on existing approaches to the problem.

8. Project description

a) *Size* — Define the geographic area to be served. Provide any relevant demographic data, e.g., number of senior citizens, schools or families in area.

b) *Target groups* — Who will be the beneficiaries of the project (groups and individuals)? Why were they chosen? How *specifically* do you plan to serve or involve them?

c) *Management* — Describe the project's day-to-day methods of supervision and support. Who is accountable to whom from bottom to top? How does the project report on its overall progress and how often and to whom? Where is your project office(s) located and why?

d) *Personnel* — State the qualifications or special training required of current and proposed staff. Outline the same for volunteers. Outline any in-service or on-the-job training provided by your project.

e) *Evaluation* — What methods will you use to evaluate the project?

Who will carry out this responsibility?

f) *Other* — Insert any information unique to this project.

9. *Budget* (See pages 96-99.)

10. *Future funding*

Funding sources want to know how you will continue your project when their grant runs out. Present a plan showing how your project will be maintained after the completion of their grant. (This section of your brief is not necessary for one-time-only grants for equipment, etc.)

One way is to show that your project will become self-sufficient through fees for service, membership, etc. Another way is to show that a local government or institution will agree to support your project if it produces the desired results. Get this kind of commitment in writing and attach it to your brief.

11. *Suggested appendices*

- last year's audited budget statement (if there is one).
- a full list of the names of your board of directors (or your policy-setting group), with addresses and telephone numbers.
- an outline of various work groups (or special committees) and task forces answering directly to your board. *Use diagrams if possible.*
- a brief history of your group.
- specially written letters of support from known and creditable persons and organizations. When asking for these, give a point-form outline of desired contents to their authors.
- any brochures or other promotional material used year-round.
- any appropriate newspaper clippings.
- if you are a performing group, attach tape cassettes of a performance inside the front cover of a ring binder.
- insert any photographs of your work, if not contained in your brochures.

General notes

- Don't mess around! Isolate yourself for whatever time is needed to write the brief in full.
- Ask for comments on your draft brief from other work groups; e.g., communications, and program planning and evaluation.
- Ask at least six complete outsiders to read over the draft of your brief. The six should be (in the following sequence):
- a professional writer and editor;

- a top secretary to check spelling, layout, etc.;
- an expert in the field to which the brief addresses itself;
- an accountant;
- a public relations professional to examine the overall package and presentation;
- someone typical of those to whom the brief will be presented.
- Remember the importance of tactile (touch) and visual impact. Make sure your brief is attractively and practically presented.
- Never overdo the packaging. You want to look professional and efficient, but not wealthy. Think "lean."
- An architect's office usually can give examples of layout, printing, diagrams and illustrations, not to mention ideas for how to cover and/or bind your brief. They may do the work for free.
- Using separating sheets for each major section is helpful. Each separating sheet should have a protruding tag at the side with the section title on it. This enables the reader to go straight to a section of interest.
- For a long brief, the most significant pages (particularly the synopsis) should be tagged at the top with the suggestion that the reader photostat and circulate these to other people who may take part in deciding whether or not your group's requests will be met.

Covering letter

Your brief must have a covering letter which:
- summarizes the contents of your brief and refers the reader to the synopsis in your brief. Most funding sources want to know that you have thoroughly planned your project, but don't want to read all the supporting material.
- makes a specific request (for funds, materials, etc.).
- asks that your proposal be returned when it has been used. This will save you money if you need to present it elsewhere.
- is signed by the most senior person in your group, or by a well-known citizen involved with your group (this will flatter the reader).

Good Reading

Jean Brodsky, ed. *The Proposal Writer's Swipe File*. Taft Products, Inc., 1000 Vermont Avenue, N.W., Washington, D.C., 20005, 1973. Twelve professionally written grant proposals, showing different ways of stating the problem, describing the proposed program, and clearly presenting a budget.

Management and Fund Raising Centre. "Grant Proposal Checklist," 1977. One of a series of how-to pamphlets, "Organizing Your Way to Dollars." $1.50 each. Can be ordered from the Centre at 287 MacPherson Avenue, Toronto, Ontario M4V 1A4.

The budget

(Appendix I of your brief)

> *Illusion is the first of all pleasures.*
> Voltaire

Why budget?

The budgeting process is a useful way of defining your group's priorities and goals. It also helps you use your money efficiently. (See also "Bookkeeping" in Chapter 7.)

What are the benefits?

Once the yearly expenditures for certain items have been set, they act as a measure (or control) of the rate of expenditure and the maximum expenditure allowed per item. When measured regularly, a too-great rate of expenditure can be corrected before it's too late. At year-end, the amount allocated per item can be compared with actual expenditures. This will show if more or less is needed for next year.

The mechanics of budgeting

1. Define the various projects or operations which should be budgeted for.
2. The amounts budgeted for each item must be realistic. Padded (high) budget projections to get more money are regarded as irresponsible. Low projections are regarded in the same light.
3. Budget for anticipated revenues using last year's figures.
4. If you are requesting support for one item of your budget, e.g., a special project, show the total figure on a separate sheet.
5. Involve those who will be spending the money in planning the amounts. You need their knowledge, and this is the only way to get their commitment to not overspend.
6. If no one in your group has experience in budgeting, find someone to help you, e.g., an accountant firm or another community group's budget expert.

Sample budget
(Cash Basis)
Fiscal Year Ended December 31, 1973
EXPENDITURES

Operating	$	$
Salaries and Professional Fees (Gross— includes Employee Benefits)—Schedule A		30,000
Utilities—Schedule B		1,000
Travel—Schedule C		500
Maintenance—Schedule D		2,500
Expendable Items—Schedule E		6,500
Rent		3,600
Insurance, Interest, Exchange and Taxes		1,000
In-Service Training and Other Operating Expenses		1,500
		46,600
Capital		
Furniture and Equipment	1,000	
Pickup Truck—½ ton (Used)	2,400	
		3,400
Total Expenditures		50,000

INCOME

Donations Solicited	1,600	
Rent	3,600	
Guests Fees	8,000	
Proceeds from Sales of Novelties	1,800	
Grant—Municipality A	15,000	
Grant—Community Service Agency	12,000	
		42,000
Estimated Excess of Expenditures Over Income for Year		8,000
Total funds requested from this source		8,000

Schedule A		
J. Jones—Administrator and Manager	11,000	
B. Brown—Social Worker	7,000	
W. White—Houseman and Cook	6,000	
G. Green, M.D.—General Physician —on call	6,000	
		30.000

Schedule B

Heat	500	
Water	100	
Electricity	200	
Telephone	200	
		1,000

Schedule C

Travel Expenses	200	
Gas and Oil for Truck	300	
		500

Schedule D

Janitorial Services	1,000	
Repairs to Roof	400	
Redecorating Rooms	1,100	
		2,500

Schedule E

Food	5,200	
Cooking Utensils	500	
Office Supplies	600	
Cleaning Supplies	200	
		6,500

Source: John Fisher. *Guide to Potential Sources of Assistance to Citizen Groups.* Toronto: Ontario Department of the Provincial Secretary and Citizenship, 1970.

Good Reading

Management and Fund Raising Centre. "How to Budget," 1977. One of a series of how-to pamphlets, "Organizing Your Way to Dollars." $1.50 each. Can be ordered from the Centre at 287 MacPherson Avenue, Toronto, Ontario M4V 1A4.

Malvern Cross, Jr. *Financial and Accounting Guide for Non-Profit Organizations.* The Ronald Press Company, 79 Madison Avenue, New York, N.Y., 10016, 1974.

Thomas F. Miller and G.R. Orser. *You Don't Know What You Got Until You Lose It.* The Support Center, 1424 16th Street N.W., Suite 201, Washington, D.C., 20036. An introduction to accounting, budgeting and tax planning for small nonprofit organizations and community groups. (See also p. 121.)

You should know about . . .

*Men take only their needs into
consideration — never their abilities.*
Napoleon Bonaparte

The following pages contain valuable information on topics related to your resource development program. Make sure you read them carefully and discuss them within your resource development group.

Membership

*True leadership is the art of changing a group from
what it is to what it ought to be.*
Virginia Allan

Why have membership?
Your group's membership is an important political and financial resource, as well as a source of volunteers. Your membership gives you:
- a head count to show the number of people concerned about the issue your group supports. This can be especially important when you are trying to convince politicians.
- a group of people who can be further educated about what you are trying to achieve, and who individually may promote your goals in the community.
- a group of people to attend a rally or demonstration, write letters to politicians, etc.
- a group of concerned people from whom you can select volunteers to fill various positions.
- a source of revenue, through membership fees, to support your group's operations.
- a sounding board for your plans and actions.

Recruiting members
1. Determine your membership needs. What talents does your group need and what areas of the community should be represented?
2. Take a member opinion survey. Ask your current members why they joined your group, what part of your program has the greatest appeal, what changes they would suggest, etc. Make sure your program is meeting your members' needs.
3. Decide on the type of new members campaign. If you need only a

few new members, perhaps a year-round effort would be best. If you need a large number of people (for example, if you are starting a new project), then an intensive campaign is called for.

4. Decide on the methods of recruiting which are most compatible with the kind of people you want. Personal visits, telephone calls, direct mail, publicity (including press releases sent to local media), advertising and guest meetings are some ways of recruiting. Ask other organizations who have held successful membership campaigns how they did it.

5. Your campaign should have a theme that will give it instant identity. Make up a short slogan and include it in all your printed material.

6. Remember, your best advertisement is your current membership. Ask them to suggest names of prospects.

Orientation

Well-informed members are likely to become active. A simple fact sheet or pamphlet will help tell your story to prospective and new members. This should explain:

- the need for your group;
- its history;
- its achievements so far;
- current programs;
- future plans;
- management structure;
- how policies are set;
- members' responsibilities (dues, voting, etc.);
- how members can help (a list of projects they can become involved in).

Attach copies of your group's publications, if any (see Chapter 10).

Try to get new members involved in specific activities right away. But remember, not all members wish to be active on committees, etc. Some show their support in a financial way.

Keeping in touch

A maintained mailing list is next to useless unless used regularly. You need an informed membership who will respond when asked. Therefore, the techniques you use to stay in touch with your membership are *vitally important*. Among these the major ones are:

- monthly bulletins, newsletters, and new publications;
- membership discussion groups and social get-togethers;

- the annual meeting.

Impress upon your members that they can make a real contribution to your group — that they are needed. Build their sense of belonging and loyalty to your group. Be sure they receive recognition for jobs well done.

Membership fees

Your membership fees must be calculated with care. If you simply require a membership for reasons 1-4 above, then a fee should be set to only cover the cost of servicing an individual member.

Membership can be used as a source of revenue starting the second year. The reason is that the cost of renewing a membership is much less than the cost of recruiting a new member. You should calculate as follows:

First year:	Cost of recruiting new member	$ 3.50
	Cost of administering new member's application, including materials (e.g. membership card)	3.50
	Cost of servicing a member (e.g. monthly magazine plus other mailing)	3.00
	Total cost of membership to member	$10.00
Second year:	Cost of requesting renewal fees	$ 1.00
	Cost of administrating renewal, including materials	1.50
	Cost of servicing member for one year	3.00
	Actual cost of membership	5.50
	Cost of membership to member	10.00
	Fund raising surplus	$ 4.50

Note: These figures are based on one experience only. Estimate your own costs based on local conditions.

Good Reading

Management and Fund Raising Centre. "A Membership Campaign," 1977. One of a how-to pamphlet series, "Organizing Your Way to Dollars." $1.50 each. Can be ordered from the Centre at 287 MacPherson Avenue, Toronto, Ontario M4V 1A4.

Membership Handbook. The Sperry Hutchinson Company, 2900 W. Seminary Drive, Fort Worth, Texas, 76133.

March Membership Enrollment Campaign Guide. The American National Red Cross, National Headquarters, Washington, D.C., 20006.

> *Life is an exciting business,*
> *and most exciting when it is*
> *lived for others.*
> Unknown

The professional fund raising firm

> *Show me a rich fortune teller.*
> Leonard Lewis Levinson

For major fund raising campaigns, the professional fund raiser can be invaluable. However, an informal survey of the experiences of citizen groups using these firms suggests caution. Here are some suggestions to help you when looking over this prospect.

1. Shop around to get as many quotes as you can from firms in your area and elsewhere. They may be listed in the Yellow Pages under Fund Raising Organizations.
2. Review the quotes and select a short list.
3. Obtain a least four in-depth references on each organization, from previous clients.
4. Most fund raising organizations will tell you they operate on a set fee and not a percentage of the total raised. This is presented as a protection for you. Nonsense. Most fund raising campaigns fail to meet their goals — not exceed them. You can end up paying a set fee for a campaign that reaches only a quarter of the agreed goal. Negotiate to pay a set fee on the condition that it does not exceed 17 percent of any total actually raised. The original set fee quoted by a fund raising firm should not exceed 10 percent of the agreed campaign goal.
5. Be wary of low quotes. What does the firm require from you⁰
   - to hire additional support staff?
   - to find volunteers to carry out the campaign?
   - to rent additional office equipment?
   - to use your office space as their campaign headquarters? This is usually a no-no, as it is sure to disrupt our regular operations.

   Add the costs of all this to the fee.
6. Firms who quote a short-term campaign period, such as one

month preparation, one month campaign, and one month followup, must be able to justify it clearly. For example, most followup work takes a minimum of two if not three months.

7. The person making the presentation may not be working on the campaign. Ask this person who the workers will be, their fund raising experience and other credentials. Ask for permission to check this information.

8. Contact a local Better Business Bureau or equivalent for their information on a fund raising firm.

9. The firm's campaign plan should have information about all of the following areas:
   - campaign leadership (organization chart);
   - campaign policies and how the campaign will conduct itself in the community;
   - methods of approaching local and national corporations, foundations, local business, individuals, employee groups, local clubs and organizations, the general public. Size of donations estimated from each type of donor — check this with other recent fund raising campaigns;
   - publicity;
   - schedule;
   - budget.

10. If the firm wishes to charge you a large sum ($1,000 to $3,000) to write a campaign plan, ask to see one they have written for a former client. The chances are this can be adapted to fit your needs, thus saving you money.

11. Insist on a contract that clearly outlines your agreement. Have it okayed by your lawyer before signing.

12. Remember that even with a fund raising firm, it is usually you who does the work — the firm is simply an advisor. Check the extent of the fund raising firms's involvement compared with your own. Have this confirmed in writing.

Special fund raising events

*Consider the postage stamp: its usefulness
consists in the ability to stick to one thing
till it gets there.*
Josh Billings

Special fund raising events are a major way of informing the public about your group and its program. They:

- create an interest in your group,
- dramatize a program,
- involve new volunteers with your group,
- strengthen morale and co-operation within your group,
- raise funds.

Special events are numerous and the results varied. Typical fund raising events are:
- bowlathons, skatathons, telethons, etc.;
- church bakes;
- card evenings;
- auctions;
- rummage sales;
- lotteries.

Typical groups to ask for information are:
- the Big Brother movement;
- service clubs;
- art galleries;
- symphonies;
- religious organizations;
- other national service organizations, for example the Multiple Sclerosis Society.

We recommend you mail your own form letter and questionnaire to other organizations (nationwide) asking for information about their fund raising efforts. The most important questions to ask are:
- What is the cost of the event (in financial and human terms)?
- What are the planning procedures and schedules?
- What are the risks?
- What were the dollar returns?
- What other information is worth knowing?

Before you plan a fund raising event, keep the following points in mind.

1. These events usually require an enormous amount of organizational work. This can dangerously drain your resources. Hence, try to find a group in the community who will run the project for you, or a group within your own group which will not be seriously diverted away from direct programs or other responsibilities.
2. These projects, like all funding efforts that involve the public, tend to expose you to your community. They should be selected and operated with the idea that your image is being created by them.
3. The majority of special events prove to be an invaluable public relations tool, but do not necessarily raise substantial funds.

Good Reading

Management and Fund Raising Centre, "Special Fund Raising Events," 1977. One of a how-to series of pamphlets, "Organizing Your Way to Dollars." $1.50 each. Can be ordered from the Centre at 287 MacPherson Avenue, Toronto, Ontario M4V 1A4.

Edwin R. Leibert and Bernice E. Sheldon. *Handbook of Special Events for Non-Profit Organizations.* New York: Association Press, 1972. An indispensable book covering:
- importance of the event;
- planning and promotion of special events;
- the long-range perspective;
- expense underwriting and sponsorship;
- examples of corporate sponsorship;
- various types of fund raising events.

Fellows, Margaret M. & Stella A. Koenig. *Tested Methods of Raising Money.* New York: Harper & Brothers, 1959.

Musselman, Virginia W., *Money Raising Activities for Community Groups,* New York: Association Press, 1969.

Pledges

Regardless of your group's size, consider "the pledge" as an important strategy. Pledges are used by United Way and other organizations to canvass large employee groups (payroll deductions), organizations and individuals who give postdated cheques or agree to be invoiced throughout the year. One hundred dollars given in three payments is regarded as "painless" giving. The longest you can expect for a corporation pledge is three years.

Pledges raise an increased amount with fewer solicitations, over a year or several-year period. Capital fund raising campaigns are especially successful using this technique.

OPEN CIRCLE THEATRE (INC.)
15 PROSPECT STREET, TORONTO M4X 1C7

A PROFESSIONAL NON-PROFIT ORGANIZATION
REGISTERED IN THE PROVINCE OF ONTARIO.
INCOME TAX REGISTRATION NUMBER 0416669-22-13
(FOR INCOME TAX DEDUCTION PURPOSES)

NAME

ADDRESS

*BEFORE PLEDGING
READ REVERSE*

PLEASE PRINT

METHOD OF PAYMENT	TERMS OF PAYMENT	
	☐ 12 monthly instalments	MY TOTAL DONATION $.
	☐ 6 monthly instalments	
☐ CASH or ☐ CHEQUE	☐ 4 quarterly instalments	MY CASH PLEDGE OR DOWN PAYMENT $.
☐ PAY DIRECT	☐ monthly	BALANCE DUE $.

Unless otherwise specified, you will be sent a reminder(s).

☐ or as follows

make cheques payable to:
OPEN CIRCLE THEATRE INC.
(post-dated cheques preferred)

DONOR'S
SIGNATURE _____ DATE _____ 1975

OPEN CIRCLE THEATRE (INC.) REQUIRED FOR PLEDGE CONTRIBUTIONS

WHY PLEDGE DOLLARS TO OPEN CIRCLE?

THIS THEATRE IS DEDICATED TO:

(a) Providing top quality theatrical entertainment. Mostly our productions set out to examine issues of local, national and international concern.

(b) Increasing the public's awareness of live theatre as a means of enriching and interpreting day to day life.

(c) Implementing programmes which expand and diversify our audience.

(d) Securing a permanent home (theatre).

The above is a simplified outline of **Open Circle's** basic objectives. During the past two years we have moved closer to achieving these aims. We still have a long way to go and need YOUR help.
You are invited to examine our artistic achievements in addition to our audience development programmes and services to the community.

AS A SPECIAL GESTURE OF SUPPORT MAY WE ASK YOU TO CONTRIBUTE TO OUR "FOUNDERS" CAMPAIGN

The minimum pledge is $100.00

NOTE: All Open Circle budgets are assembled and supervised by Open Circle Theatre Management in collaboration with Philip Mathews, C.A. of the Clarkson Gordon Company.

Sample pledge card

Direct mail campaign

Asking for donations in a letter sent to a large number of people may produce a dependable source of income for your group. Research shows that people who have donated by mail continue to do so consistently over the years. (See "Fund Raising Letters" on page 79, and "How to Write a Brief" on page 92.)

A direct mail campaign is successful if you take in more money than you spend to do the mailing (writing and printing the letters, postage, pre-paid reply envelopes, etc.).

There are two approaches:
- mailing to your donor base — your list of people who have donated before to your group,
- mailing to other people, to recruit new donors.

107

Mailings to the donors one has acquired almost always is a money-making proposition (15-30 percent return). Mailings to cold prospects rarely is (1-2 percent is the usual return on any new mailing). However, it is worth spending money to acquire new donors, because of their value as future donors.

People to mail your letters to include:

- previous donors;
- members of your group;
- readers of your group's newsletter, annual report, etc.;
- interested community people, such as those who have attended your public meetings;
- donor or other mailing lists from other organizations who have similar or related aims — consider enclosing your letter in one of their mailings;
- people in professions, government, whom your group has contact with;
- subscriber lists for publications whose subject matter indicates the type of person who might donate to your group.

The payoff is not immediate. Depending on the method of building your lists, it takes two to four years for direct mail lists to become profitable.

Follow these guidelines for a successful direct mail campaign.

1. You're on safer ground with many small donors than with a few large donors.
2. Low-cost mailing rates are available to nonprofit organizations. Normally you must have applied for and received tax-exempt status from the IRS. For information about procedure, ask your post office for Publication #13. Approval for a mailing permit can take up to a year.
3. Send your thankyou's and tax receipts to donors *as soon as possible*. A donor's suspicion of your group grows if he must wait a long time for a response from you.
4. Keep track of the cost and response to your mail campaign, and evaluate its effectiveness.
5. If you feel you must use the services of a direct mail agency (which has mailing lists of its own), choose it carefully. Look for success in your particular field of activity. How long did it take to show a donor profit? What is the cost-contribution ratio? Size of list and frequency of mailings?

To find out more about direct mailing, contact the Direct Mail Fund Raisers Association, 810 Seventh Ave., New York, N.Y. 10019.

Good Reading
Mitchell Keller, ed. *The KRC Guide to Direct Mail Fund Raising.*
KRC Development Council, 212 Elm Street, New Canaan,
Connecticut 06840. The most recent and best publication on direct
mail fund raising.

Tax incentives

*When a fellow says, "It ain't the money
but the principle of the thing,"
it's the money.*
Kim Hubbard

Current tax regulations allow an individual to donate up to 50 percent
of his adjusted gross income to tax-exempt organizations and claim
these donations as deductions from income. The average American
pays roughly 10 percent of his income in federal income taxes.
Therefore, if a person makes a donation of $100, he is actually making
a personal contribution of $90. The remainder would have been paid
as tax, so in effect it is a donation by the federal government. (Of
course this varies with the percentage of income paid in taxes.) In this
manner an individual can redirect his tax dollars. This applies only if
he has given his money to a group or organization whose activities are
essentially educational, religious, scientific or philanthropic. He may
not claim deductions for contributions to groups whose major
purpose is to effect changes in the law or government policy.

The same is true for corporate deductions. Most large corporations
are in high tax brackets. It is to their advantage to reduce their net
incomes so their tax bracket is lower. However, they can claim
deductions only up to 5 percent of net income. Not that they have
been strongly tempted to surpass this limit: total corporate deductions
in 1973 amounted to only 0.75 percent of net corporate income.

The 1969 Tax Reform Act restricted many of the former advantages
of setting up a foundation. At present the law requires a foundation to
distribute annually an amount equal to at least 5 percent of the fair
market value of its shares and other holdings. In other words,
foundations are expected to disburse all their investment income,
retaining only as much money as they need to operate.

Gifts to government at any level are subject to the same limits of 50
percent of individual and 5 percent of corporate income that apply to
gifts to private organizations. Gifts may be made only to agencies that

will use them for public purposes. Contact a district IRS Center for more information.

Tax receipts may be given for gifts of goods and property; it is up to the donor to justify the value he assigns to his gift to the IRS. It is *not* allowable to claim deductions for donated services. Nor can your organization issue receipts for the rent-free use of office space or other facilities.

Reserve fund

If possible, start a reserve fund for rainy days. Pay an amount into it each year. If you launch a fund raising drive, add an amount to its goal to be used as an interest-earning reserve fund. Obtain the voluntary services of an accountant to determine how much of your funds you should use in this way.

The diversified funding base

This term means keeping your sources of financial support quite separate from each other. It is simply a way of protecting your group from the danger of a single funding source lessening or ending its support. This is particularly needed for citizen groups which have a more

110

contentious advocacy role, particularly when they are doing their job well.

Another aspect is control. For example, is an organization truly an independent member of the private sector simply because its board of directors consists of citizens, when 90 percent to 100 percent of its funds come from government? Too much accommodating the hand that feeds you is a dangerous thing!

Others who should know

Before your fund raising reaches into the community, make sure your local Chamber of Commerce and Better Business Bureau are aware of:
- who your group is;
- what your resource development aims are;
- what you plan to do with any donations.

If you are conducting a more widespread community campaign, such as door-to-door solicitation, it is important to inform your local police department as well. Make certain all people soliciting for you are listed at your main office and can provide on-the-spot identification of their involvement with your group.

Good Reading
"Standards for Charitable Solicitation," Council of Better Business Bureaus, Inc. Washington, D.C., 1974.

Build or spread?

In times of restraint, when funding sources cannot keep pace with requests for funds, they must decide whether to "build or spread."

"Build" means giving to the same number of groups or to fewer, but giving each more each year. "Spread" means to fund an increasing number of groups, giving each group less.

The debate is a serious one and difficult to resolve. Don't hesitate to ask your sources of funds for their stance on this issue, so you know where *you* stand!

Cost sharing

The federal government engages in a variety of cost sharing and fund matching programs with other levels of government, universities,

111

research establishments, corporations, and nonprofit organizations. If you can obtain part of your funding from other sources, the government may be willing to provide the rest. Arrangements vary from agency to agency; in some cases only a token contribution is required of the grantee. General policies in this area are described in Federal Management Circular 73-3, available from the Office of Management Policy of the General Services Administration, 18 and F Streets N.W., Washington, D.C. 20405.

Project financing

Alas, I am dying beyond my means.
Oscar Wilde

Many funding sources are reluctant to give support to the ongoing operations of an organization. Rather, they prefer to give grants to *separate* short-term projects. The following should help you to understand their reasoning.
1. They see response to new needs and issues as the private sector's primary responsibility.
2. A specific project reassures them their money is being spent in an area they judge to be important. Funding sources are becoming suspicious that too much "fat" is tolerated in ongoing administration.
3. Specific project funding is more measurable.
4. Government funding sources are reluctant to become committed to a program forever, without the option to pull out.
5. Long-term projects over a period of years can lose their effectiveness as community needs change.
   All this has created a crisis for groups which carry large overheads of professional and secretarial staff, offices, etc. Ways to lessen the drain that overhead has on your group are:
- trim all possible "fat" from your operations;
- divide your existing operations or programs into projects and seek funding for these (see the hub and spokes model, below).

How not to cut back

The best you get is an even break.
Franklin Adams

Continuing activities such as publicity or community development, etc., each with its own staff and volunteers, are usually regarded as a group's ongoing program. This type of program is financed from the (ongoing) operations budget.

When financing deteriorates, groups "cut back" on these programs. *This is self-defeating!* It is the impact of your programs that gains a reputation for your group; and your reputation, in turn, generates funds and other resources.

So look over all your ongoing programs to see if, with some changes, they can be individually packaged and sold as projects. Write a brief for each existing program revamped as a project, building an amount into its budget to cover the cost of any services it receives from your ongoing overhead, e.g., rent, professional consultation, secretarial services, supervision, bookkeeping, etc. The portion of support services diverted into each project should not exceed 13 percent of the total project cost.

The hub and spokes model

How to divide your existing operations into projects: Start by drawing your own hub and spokes outline. Then take your ongoing general

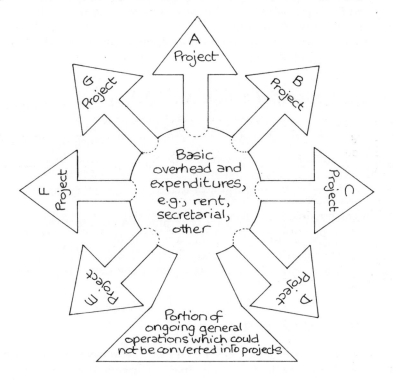

operations and overhead, and convert as many as you can into special project thrusts (the spokes). Remember, special project funding terminates after one or two years. Think how you are going to cope from that point on — a yearly campaign?

Note: Each project uses 10% of its budget to purchase support services from the "hub" or ongoing general operations base.

When arranging project financing, keep the following points in mind.
1. Designing *new* projects and presenting briefs only to chase money may have the effect of pulling your organization away from its original goals.
2. Be careful. Even though your program staff and volunteers probably are most concerned about shortages of dollars and other resources, try not to involve them too closely with resource development because they:
   - may not possess any aptitude or ability in the resource development area; and consequently
   - may have a frustrating experience with fund raising, which would demoralize them for any further program or resource development work; and
   - they should not be taken away from their programs, which are the lifeblood of any group.

Revenue potential within your group

You should give people the opportunity to contribute to the cost of your services, if they are able. For example, you can include a solicitation for membership or an invoice with brochures being mailed. For public education courses, you either can charge a nominal fee at the door, or request an honorarium (a token amount) from the original sponsor.

In other words, look at all your programs and see if there is revenue potential in them. However, be sure any fees you charge will not exclude people you are trying to reach. Be sure to estimate the total projected revenues and see if the costs of collecting them make it worth your while.

The forgivable loan

When your group's finances dry up and when you have submitted applications for funds, it may be possible to secure a forgivable loan (a loan you don't have to pay back if you can't). Another large community organization may be willing to provide a small, interest-free "bridging" loan. It is important that these funds are negotiated on a forgivable basis in the event your expected funds do not materialize. The person or organization providing the loan must be made fully aware of the risks involved. All arrangements of this nature must include signed agreements between the two parties.

The loan

When your group has received confirmation of a grant or other income, another community organization can either arrange to give you a repayable loan or they can co-sign for you to secure a bank loan. As a general principle, plan ahead and operate on a cash basis (only spend what you have). Get an iron-clad guarantee for the funds (in writing from the person who has the authority to give such assurance) before starting any action based on the funds.

Speaking engagements

> *If you don't strike oil in twenty minutes*
> *stop boring.*
> Andrew Carnegie

As well as educating the community about your group or a particular issue, the speaking engagement is a wonderful introduction to resources. Note that etiquette dictates you ask permission from your host before you solicit your audience.

At the conclusion of your speech, describe your resource development program. Then pass around your shopping list (bring enough copies). Make certain your name and address are attached to it. If, on the other hand, you are requesting (or challenging) the audience as an organization to take on a project for your group, leave your shopping list at home.

Presentations and deputations

These differ slightly from the speaking engagement: you are quite definitely asking for something.

It is always advisable to bring an easy-to-read flip chart with short sentences and diagrams to highlight your presentation. You should

115

give a miniature of your flip chart to each person in your audience (unless it is too large). You can use other visual aids, including slides and film. However, be sensitive to the time that your audience (e.g., a local council) can give to your presentation or deputation, and plan accordingly. If you use electronic aids to your presentation, make sure that:
- your equipment works;
- you set it up before the audience enters the room;
- you have a skilled operator on hand.

If you can, discuss your upcoming presentation with two or three persons to whom the presentation will be made. This is a way of "fine tuning" your presentation to better fit the biases of those listening. Also attempt to secure the support of one or two or the most respected listeners before the presentation. They may come to the meeting already prepared with motions to support your request. Suggest that they do this.

Good Reading
Ray J. Friant, Jr. *Preparing Effective Presentations — How to Make a Presentation Pay Off.* Pilot Industries, 347 Fifth Avenue, New York, N.Y., 10016, 1971. A guide to constructing a visually aided oral presentation. Describes the sequence and content of presentation, strategy, outline, storyboard, rough and finished visuals, with hints on presentation.

> *A man who cannot seduce men*
> *cannot save them either.*
> Soren Kierkegaard

Deferred giving (bequests)

A notice which reads as follows should be displayed on all your literature:

"Over the years, many people have chosen to perpetuate their support of (name of your group) through a bequest in their will. Sometimes these are directed specifically to (name one or two of your better known programs) or to (name of your group) as a whole.

"You or your legal advisor may wish to contact us for any further information."

Include the name and address of someone they can contact.

Make certain all local lawyers are on your regular mailing list and, if possible, become members of your group. Lawyers are consulted about worthwhile community groups by persons preparing wills and may pass on available information about your group.

Contact lawyers in your area to see if there is a legal directory in which you can purchase space. Use it to encourage lawyers to mention your group to their clients when they are drawing up wills. It is important you include the name of your group, its purpose, and the name and telephone number of a contact person who can deal with enquiries from lawyers.

Make certain you contact them once each year to make sure they are aware of your group and your desire to receive bequests.

Ask them about donations through:
- wills;
- life insurance;
- living trusts;
- estate planning;
- memorial gifts.

The best way to get bequests for your group is to have two or three people round up twenty or thirty more. Each writes three letters to friends, asking them to remember your group in their wills. This method is indirect enough to be discreet, yet direct enough to bring results.

Good Reading
Management and Fund Raising Centre. "Guide to Deferred Giving," 1977. One of a series of how-to pamphlets "Organizing Your Way to Dollars." $1.50 each. Can be ordered from the Centre at 287 MacPherson Avenue, Toronto, Ontario M4V 1A4.

A New Dimension for United Funds. United Community Funds and Councils of America, 345 Each 46 Street, New York, New York 10017. Describes how to set up a deferred giving (bequest) program.

Special occasion donation cards

Donation cards for special occasions are another way people can donate to your group.

Such a card goes something like this:
"For your (aniversary, birthday, in memoriam, get well, bon voyage, etc.), in lieu of flowers or a gift, I have sent $_____ to (name of your organization and a brief description of what it does, perhaps with an interesting photograph). (Space for the donor's name.)"

117

Your group prints these cards and sells them (to your members, through funeral parlours and hospitals, which often have racks of cards from many charities, etc.) for anywhere from $2-$15. This is in effect a donation from the buyer. One charitable group sells a card which includes a 4'' x 5'' gold frame for $18.

Keep track of these donors and list their names every few months in your newsletter.

A variation is a temporary fund for your group which is set up to honour someone or in memoriam. People telephone or send their donations. When the donation period is finished, the person or family who set up the fund decides how they want the money to be spent.

7

Management (administration) work group

It is not enough to have great qualities,
we should also have the management of them.
La Rochefoucauld

The role of a management work group is to find ways to operate an organization efficiently and effectively. In simple terms, it determines *how* an organization can best reach its goal, *who* is going to do it, *what* resources are needed (human, financial, other) and, finally, *how long* it will take. Administration is organizing the details of getting these things done.

No matter how small or large your organization, basic management operations include:
- outlining a course of action and schedule of activities — what exactly needs to be done;
- selecting the people to do the jobs;
- assigning duties;
- training those people;
- bringing together human and material resources;
- general support of personnel;
- maintaining adequate records and reports;
- budgeting;
- assessing methods used to evaluate progress.

These and other functions make up the operations part of an organization. Some of these activities are discussed in this section — others are discussed elsewhere in the manual.

119

We strongly urge you to approach a government, a university or a corporation to borrow a management expert, without cost. This person can help you set up an effective management system. Make sure he understands your area of interest and its unique demands.

Facts, apart from their relationships,
are like labels on empty bottles.
Sven Italla

120

Good Reading

Robert N. Anthony and Regina E. Herzlinger. *Management Control in Non-Profit Organizations*. Homewood, Illinois: Richard D. Irwin, Inc., 1975.

Bookkeeping

> *Creditor: a man who has a better memory than a debtor.*
>
> Unknown

Once you have secured financial resources, it is imperative you set up bookkeeping procedures to keep track of your revenues and expenditures.

Useful books include:

Malvern Cross, Jr. *Financial and Accounting Guide for Non-Profit Organizations*. The Ronald Press Company, 79 Madison Avenue, New York, New York 10016, 1974.

Thomas F. Miller and G.R. Orser. *You Don't Know What You Got Until You Lose It*. The Support Center, 1424 16th Street N.W., Suite 201, Washington, D.C. 20036, 1975.

If you need instructions on how to set up a detailed "functional budget," read:

Standards of Accounting and Financial Reporting for Voluntary Health and Welfare Organizations. National Health Council, 1740 Broadway, New York, New York 10019.

However, the most comprehensive guide available is:

Accounting and Financial Reporting. United Ways of America, Systems, Planning and Allocations Division, 801 Fairfax Street, Alexandria, Virginia 22314. A guide for United Ways and nonprofit human service organizations.

When setting up your financial books, obtain the advice of an accountant. Certified public accountants will consult free as a public service to nonprofit organizations. It is important that during your first year your financial advisors check in detail your bookkeeping on at least three occasions. Much of a group's reputation can rest on its financial management. Don't skirt in this area. If necessary, hire a part-time bookkeeper on an hourly rate. Don't carry out a single transaction until a competent person is in full control of your books.

OUTLINE OF A PROGRESS CHART

← 10 ft →

Name of Project	Jan	Feb	Mar	Apr	May	June	July	Aug	Sept	Oct	Nov	Dec	Other Definition
													e.g., a priority rating and what organizational objectives are being met by the project (See the yearly agenda)

↕ 8 ft

Name of Project This, like all postings on the progress chart should be boldly displayed. A descriptive paragraph may be added, in small printing. Each card should be approximately 3 inches high by 1 foot across.

Time Frame Each month should state the goal to be achieved at that time. If a project falls behind schedule, a large red arrow should be pinned to the month in question. Too many red arrows suggest that the project may have problems or that scheduling expectations were unrealistic and rescheduling is in order.

Notes

1. Progress charts must be large and easy to read.
2. They must be displayed wherever and whenever your policy-setting group meets.
3. One person should be solely responsible for the updating of the chart on at least a monthly basis.
4. Although it is normal to use a progress chart to measure the progress of *overall* projects, a second progress chart can be used to measure the progress of each of the seven work groups.
5. The basic materials needed for a non-portable grid are: wood edging; cork squares; ½" ribbon; cards; magic marker.

122

Progress chart

*When a man knows he is to be hanged
in a fortnight, it concentrates his
mind wonderfully.*
Samuel Johnson

A progress chart is a simple and useful way to keep sight of your goal, and to keep everyone informed and motivated. The progress chart is a tangible schedule of your organization's activity, step by step. The chart is open to all. Everyone, including volunteers, clerical staff, professional staff, board members and visitors, is invited to question and challenge what the chart shows.

Start your policy setting meetings with a review of your progress chart. It is an important motivating force, particularly for groups dealing with intangible issues. It shows progress to date, and helps people feel they are achieving your organization's goal. Be careful, however, not to overdo it. Time can be spent measuring, constructing charts, time sheets, etc., to a point of absurdity.

There are four basics in making a progress chart:
1. Get a clear understanding of the issue, its size, its implications and what your group wishes to accomplish.
2. Decide your priorities within the issue.
3. Decide how much of the issue you can realistically take on, given your human and financial resources.
4. Plan your specific step by step objectives, and the final goal.

Remember, your policy-setting group (or board of directors) as a whole, and your management work group in particular, must consider these points at least once and preferably four times a year.

Image manipulation

Did it ever occur to you that while a donor of resources to a citizen group is in a way the buyer of its services, he is rarely the recipient or consumer of same. Because the "buyer" rarely, if ever, meets the consumer, the "buyer" relies to a large extent on what he is told by the citizen group. Progress charts and the like are outward signs that a group is managing its donated resources efficiently, and that the donor's contribution will have an impact in the community. This usually can be counted on to impress resource donors — particularly those with a limited capability for evaluating the group's programs.

However, management tools like the progress chart must be used on a day-by-day, week-by-week basis. They must not remain idle or be hurriedly updated when a funding source or other influential group visits. This is image manipulation and a serious breach of ethical standards.

Basically, the progress chart is a *quantitative* measure of your efficiency in getting things done, not a *qualitative* measure of a program's impact. It is up to your program task group to find responsible ways to measure program impact and supply this information to all those who need it. Too few organizations bother to do this. *The better the donor is educated, the more likely his donations of resources will increase.* The resource development work group, communications work group, and program planning and evaluation work group should get together to find ways of doing this. However, don't overburden the donor with too much information.

In addition, try to put your resource donors in direct contact with the people you are serving.

Corporate ingenuity

A man is known by the company he organizes.
Ambrose Bierce

Citizen groups all over the continent spend hundreds of millions of dollars yearly, yet they have stayed aloof from the mainstream of managerial science. Staff and volunteers alike learn by trial and error. This is frustrating and wasteful.

The "get it done" techniques of trade and commerce can help citizen groups improve their overall performance. Most citizen groups see the corporate ethic as at best suspect, and at worst the enemy. This is often an excuse for not co-operating with persons who can, if approached correctly, prove most helpful. Says Dr. John Frei: "Citizen organizations must always bear in mind that their task as organizations is to give to the people of our communities the largest possible quantity of service for the lowest price."

Good Reading
Seven Things Non-Profits Can Learn From Profits. J.R. Taft Corporation, 1000 Vermont Ave. N.W., Suite 6000, Washington D.C., 20005. An interesting poster. The seven things are:
1. How to get down to reality;
2. Make marketing a way of life;

3. Look at your problems through the eyes of others (you may be a little nearsighted);
4. No one can be all things to all people (find a need and fill it);
5. Find your position in life (and communicate it);
6. You must compete (because if you don't your competition will);
7. You have more to sell than you think. A little profit thinking in the nonprofit world? It's a business way of life.

Robert Townsend. *Up the Organization.* New York: Alfred A. Knopf Inc. 1970. A survival manual for corporations. Citizen groups can adapt this know-how.

Management by objectives (MBO)

Regardless of how large or small your group is, you can use the basic principles of MBO. MBO has been praised and damned by those who have applied its managerial philosophy. Dr. D. Wayland says, "It works if it is not abused by those at the top to coerce others into meeting goals that have been imposed rather than proposed. Management by objectives is in fact a concept based on democratic participation and linking tightly the four phases of the management process (planning, organizing, directing and controlling)."

The progress chart is a simple way of displaying and keeping track of the steps to achieve a pre-stated goal. MBO is a way of arriving at your goal.

See if your resource develoment work group can locate a management expert who will either provide you with a management training program or become a member of your management (administration) work group.

Good Reading
Peter F. Drucker. *The Practice of Management.* New York: Harper and Row, 1954.

George S. Odiorne. *Management by Objectives.* New York: Pitman Publishers, 1965.

The cycle of management by objectives

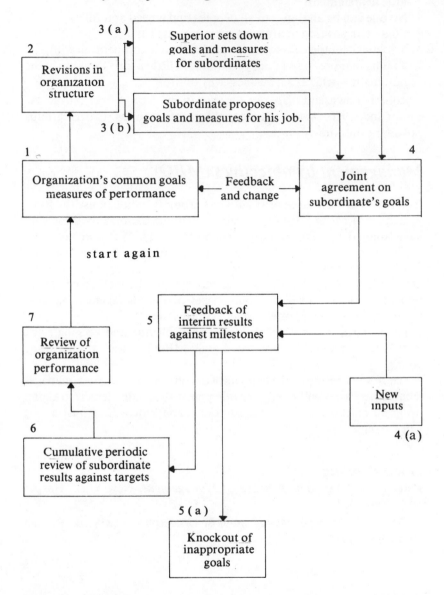

Notes on management

*Lots of folks confuse bad management
with destiny.*
Frank Hubbard

Watch out for paper! Paper is the most prevalent feature of modern organizations and, as such, should be its best servant. Use it wisely. For example, internal forms should never be created unless they can be filled out easily on a regular basis, without confusion or aggravation. Another example is memoranda. The time these take to dictate and type often is not justified by their content. Unless the message is important, speak directly, phone or scribble a note to the person you are trying to reach.

In organizations dealing with intangible issues such as mental health and social planning, there is a tendency to generate reams of unnecessary paper to give a day's work some tangible product and therefore some meaning.

Plan staff time. All staff should file in advance a simple monthly plan of objectives. These should be approved by the supervisor. At weekly planning meetings, progress should be reviewed against the plans. The supervisor reports his staff's progress to the policymakers based on these monthly reports and performance evaluations.

Why private offices? For most staff and volunteers, their need for an office is minimal. An open work space should be enough. A general meeting room can be scheduled by individuals for meetings or personal interviews. Office space costs money.

Why secretaries? Create a staff service centre with typists, for everyone that needs this service. One person, depending on volume, can cope with phone messages. If someone really needs an assistant then hire one, but don't hire a personal secretary.

8

Volunteer work group

*I've always considered statesmen
to be more expendable than soldiers.*
Unknown

Because people are such an important resource, a separate work group should be formed to recruit, train and place volunteers for all types of work within your group. To keep things simple, we described *who they are* and *where to find them* in the Resource Development Work Group section of this manual.

Why volunteers?

*The means-and-ends moralists, or
non-doers, always end up on their
ends without any means.*
Saul Alinsky

Volunteers are the most important resource of any group. In addition to their contributions, they are the embodiment of citizen participation — the community working for itself. There is nothing a paid person does that a volunteer cannot do. ∴

For most community groups and organizations, volunteers fill two categories:

Direct	— immediate and personal activity; e.g., visiting the sick, being a big brother, taking part in a demonstration, organizing minority groups, selling tickets for a function.
Indirect	— administrative and advisory activities, e.g., sitting on boards of directors, commissions, committees, where policies are set or influenced.

If your group wants to use volunteers, you first should organize a work group to deal solely with the volunteer program. This includes:

- recruiting;
- screening;
- orientation;
- placement;
- ongoing support.

This work group should define its own goals and tasks, and do the same for volunteers it plans to recruit. For a large or growing volunteer program, you should consider hiring a volunteer co-ordinator.

A volunteer co-ordinator, responsible to your volunteer work group, is a must for any volunteer program providing that the total output of the volunteers in terms of time and other contributions is more than the cost of maintaining the co-ordinator. This may not apply in the first two years of a new program.

This ratio should be assessed annually. Since one co-ordinator can recruit and support many volunteers, the ratio should be substantial. For example, for every dollar spent on the co-ordinator, six dollars should be contributed in volunteer time (and other contributions they make). An ideal program can achieve a $1 spent to $10 donated time and skills ratio!

The volunteer co-ordinator's responsibilities are to:

- find potential volunteers (see below);
- screen them for general suitability and to assess skills and motivation;
- assess where a volunteer can contribute the most;
- hold orientation and training sessions;
- organize task outlines and schedules;
- give support (one-to-one or in group meetings);
- evaluate the volunteer program;
- report regularly to the work group.

If you cannot afford a co-ordinator, you must carry out this work yourselves. See the Good Reading section at the end of this chapter for help in doing this.

129

Recruitment of volunteers

> *Recruiting volunteers is not like finding*
> *water in the desert; it is more like*
> *controlling Niagara Falls.*
>
> Ivan Scheier, National Information Center
> on Volunteerism, Inc., U.S.A.

Your aim is to recruit and *keep* as many volunteers as you need for your program. Before you start a public recruitment campaign, give a list of your volunteer needs to your local volunteer centre (if there is one in your community).

Here are some techniques for effectively reaching people. (See also Chapter 10 of this manual.)

1. *Letters.* Send letters to church groups, social organizations, schools, inactive volunteers, etc., inviting them to take part.

2. *Newspapers.* Send news items and progress reports to local newspapers, community newsletters, etc. Have local merchants sponsor a series of advertisements. The newspaper advertising salesman can find sponsors for you.
3. *Radio and TV.* Use public service announcements or arrange personal interviews and discussions on your issue or problem.
4. *Meetings.* Sponsor a volunteer rally, or invite potential volunteers to an orientation meeting.
5. *Posters.* Place them on bulletin boards of supermarkets, schools, churches, etc.
6. *Telephone campaigns.* One-to-one recruiting methods can be used. Follow up personal contacts and referrals by telephone.
7. *Brochures and fliers.* Distribute in public places and at related group meetings.
8. *Speakers.* Those who know your group well can talk about it to individuals and groups.
9. *Other methods.* Neighbourhood coffee parties, block parties, a babysitting service to attract volunteers with pre-school children, sign-up booth, handouts at conventions and meetings, an exhibit in the library. Find out if another community group will do these projects for you. (See Chapter 6 of this manual.)

Stress the personal advantages of involvement with your group when persuading volunteers to donate their services to your organization. Altruism is never the only reason people volunteer.

Whenever you select a new volunteer clearly spell out in writing his responsibilities to the organization and the organization's to him. This is called a volunteer contract. Both parties should sign this as a statement of intent.

Secondments (loaned staff) and sabbaticals (study leaves)

Government departments, corporations and universities are beginning to favour the secondment and the sabbatical. It allows them to support a citizen group without spending additional dollars. In addition, the employee volunteered learns a lot during his stay with your group.

Inquire informally first. Then decide on your approach. You can submit a brief which clearly outlines the task, and the benefits to your community and to the contributing organization. Remember, a person who works with you on secondment or sabbatical does so to gain in some way. *Emphasize how, in your request.* And don't take just anybody; make sure the person has the skills you need and can fit into your group.

Great acts are made up of small deeds.
Lao Tsu

ACTION

ACTION, the massive federal agency for volunteerism, will:
- supply volunteers at the request of community agencies;
- assist community volunteer project development;
- provide materials and technical assistance to volunteer projects.

Call ACTION toll-free at 800-425-8580 to obtain the address and telephone number of the regional director for your area. Or write to ACTION, Washington, D.C. 20525.

Good Reading

Schindler Rainman and Ronald Lippitt. *The Volunteer Community: Creative Use of Human Resources.* Second edition. Fairfax, Virginia: NTL Learning Resources Corporation, 1975.

Anne K. Stenzel and Helen M. Feeney. *Volunteer Training and Development: A Manual for Community Groups.* New York: Seabury Press, 1968.

Marlene Wilson. *The Effective Management of Volunteer Programs.* Volunteer Management Associates, 279 South Cedar Brook Road, Boulder, Colorado 80302, 1976.

Thomas A. Routh. *The Volunteer and Community Agencies.* Charles C. Thomas, Inc. 301-327 East Lawrence Avenue, Springfield, Illinois 62703, 1972.

The National Center for Voluntary Action offers many useful publications. See pages 73 and 74 of this manual.

Virtue would go far if
vanity did not keep it
company.
La Rochefoucauld

132

9

Personnel work group

*The meeting of two personalities is like
the contact of two chemical substances:
if there is any reaction, both are
transformed.*

Carl Jung

Why hire staff?

The reasons:
1. to co-ordinate volunteer effort and advise volunteers on the best ways and courses of action (policy advice);
2. to be responsible for the basic maintenance of projects and programs;
3. to provide continuity: an issue may stay alive for several years, but waves of volunteers come and go;
4. to do the detailed preparatory and administrative work in support of volunteer effort.

The dangers:
1. volunteers may abdicate their responsibilities, leaving the work to staff;
2. volunteers and staff may be unclear on their respective responsibilities, to the point of malfunction;
3. staff may stifle volunteer initiative and be incompetent in their general dealings with volunteers.

Administrator versus manager

These terms are the same — at first glance. The difference is to be learned from their origin. To administer is from the Latin *ad* meaning to and *minister* meaning servant. To manage is from the Italian *managgiare* meaning to handle (a horse) and further back from the Latin *manus* meaning hand. Therefore, when we administer, we help people accomplish their tasks, and when we manage, we lead them — in the original sense of the word — by the hand. When distinguishing between the two, Clarence King talks about "professional skill" and "executive ability."

Citizen groups, then, must select one or the other when hiring their key staff person.

Policy versus operations

Conventionally, staff or volunteers suggest a policy and a program to achieve it, to the policy-setting group. The staff await the policy setter's decision; if it is yes, staff begin the program. Policy setters have the final say in setting policies and approving program design and cost.

Often, volunteer policy setters in a citizen group will wear two hats — policy and operations. It must be clearly understood that staff are the managers (leaders) in the operations (program) area.

Who is an executive?

The abilities top staff must have in various situations are too many to list. However, we will look at some.

In 1958, *Fortune* magazine did a survey of high ranking executives in industry and commerce. The three most important qualities they found were emotional stability, integrity and dependability.

A description of the executive for Dr. John W. Frei's working paper, "The Executive and His Role in Social Service," reads:

"An executive is a leader who understands human nature and behaviour, has an extensive body of professional knowledge and skill, and uses his personality as a medium for organization of a group of people working with proper material means, in close co-operation, efficiently towards effective achievement of certain goals."

Clarence King, from "Your Community in Action," introduces his discussion on the qualities of an executive of a social welfare agency with these words:

"If our goal is to be realistic we must face the fact that seldom will we find in one human being all of the qualities that should be possessed by the ideal executive, if he is to be a wise leader of both our Board and staff. We will need him to serve as our expert advisor while we are arriving at our policy decisions, and thereafter he must have both professional skill and executive ability in carrying these policies into effect."

A question of balance

> *A man may be so much of everything*
> *that he is nothing of anything.*
> Samuel Johnson

The most important aspect of a citizen group's function is its pro-

135

grams. As a consequence, when hiring the top staff person, groups are inclined to recruit someone who is an expert in a certain program area, but who probably is not a manager.

The debate still is not settled. Should groups hire someone who can contribute much to the development of programs, or should they find a manager and developer of resources? Of course, ability as a program expert does not exclude management abilities, but as a rule the two don't mix.

You cannot develop your program without adequate and well-managed resources. On the other hand, without a good program you will not attract resources to your group.

The solution is simply one of balance. To achieve this essential balance, you can have:

- a program expert as your executive director with a manager as your assistant executive director;
- a management expert as your executive director and a program expert as your assistant executive director;
- either one of the above two options, with either a strong program planning or management work group to provide the necessary balance.

Hiring the top staff person

Duty is what one expects from others.
Oscar Wilde

When selecting a top staff person for your group, ask at least two or three experienced top staff from similar community groups or outside organizations to advise the selection process and participate in the interviewing. Apply this principle to all your hiring; e.g., ask skilled communications people when you are selecting public relations staff, etc.

Hire a person to carry out a clearly defined task or path of action — not fill a position. This task becomes the yardstick both for you and for the staff person. It can save confusion and bitterness if staff achievements are questioned.

On practical matters regarding staff, you can seek guidance from a United Way, an established community welfare group, or other organizations.

You need to decide about these things:

- job description — should you have one, and who develops it?
- how much to pay the top staff person?
- what yearly increases?

- a car with the job?
- expenses — how much? Should you set limits or have an open ended policy?
- a benefits package?
- what vacations?
- moving costs?
- separation pay?
- terminal contract or tenure?

Good Reading:

Dr. John W. Frei. *The Executive and His Role in Social Services.* A working paper. Social Planning Council of Metropolitan Toronto, 320 Bloor Street East, Toronto, Ontario, June, 1974.

Guidelines for Employment Practices by Funds and Councils. United Way of Canada/ Centraide Canada, 55 Parkdale Avenue, Ottawa, Ontario. A general guide for employers.

Ray E. Johns. *Exploring Organizational Behaviour.* School of Social Work, University of Toronto, Ontario, 1970. A detailed probe of all aspects of organization in a community group, including individuals in organizations, exploring goal concepts and worker identification and performance.

Evaluation of staff performance

It is much easier to be critical than to be correct.
Benjamin Disraeli

Methods to evaluate staff performance within humanistic fields are still being developed. One of the problems is the intangible and subjective nature of these fields. There really aren't x number of units at the end of the production line each day; nor are there other yardsticks, such as financial profit and loss.

Most organizations settle for a quantitative measure. This consists of setting objectives for the organization and for each person (including volunteers) involved with achieving them. Staff should file monthly and weekly objectives agreed upon with their supervisor. Progress against these objectives should be evaluated at a weekly meeting. If an individual is experiencing difficulties, these should be analysed and solutions found. The progress chart is an extension of this process.

For more information on one evaluation method, "The Hay System," contact: Hay Associates, Management Consultants, 1845 Walnut Street, Philadelphia, Pennsylvania 19103.

Good Reading

Hedley G. Dimock. *Planning Group Development.* Sir George Williams Bookstore, Concordia University, Montreal, Quebec, H3G 1M8, 1974. ($1.50) A guide to helping people work together, including sections on discussions, problem solving, behavioural problems, strategies for change, etc. Another book by the same author is *Factors in Working with Groups.*

10

Communications work group

*If one tells the truth, one is sure
sooner or later to be found out*
Oscar Wilde

Communications can be broken down into the two general areas of external and internal communications. External communication includes general public relations, discussed in Section A of this chapter; use of the media to promote organizational goals, treated in Section B; and communication with other groups, covered in Chapter 12. Internal communication is discussed in Section C of this chapter, which covers methods of keeping staff and volunteers informed of the activities of the organization as a whole.

Section A: Communicating with the Public

In general

*One of the large consolations for experiencing anything unpleasant
is the knowledge that one can communicate it.*
Joyce Carol Oates

The standing of your group in your community is determined by the quality of your communications. This includes explaining yourselves and bringing about change (advocacy).

EXPLANATION
OF YOUR
ORGANIZATION

COMMUNICATING
TO CHANGE
THINGS

COMMUNICATING
WITHIN THE
ORGANIZATION

To achieve good public relations:

1. You must explain your purpose, relating it to the lives of individuals in your community.
2. You must write your publicity in the language your readers use. Watch out for jargon or technical terms.
3. Every communications job needs a central theme to make it effective.
4. You must skilfully schedule your communication work group's time to meet deadlines.
5. Every person involved with your group has responsibility for its public relations. Tell them this.
6. Publicity cannot make silk purses from sows' ears. Don't oversell.
7. Developing good public relations is a year-round effort.
8. Public relations is a two-way street! Listen to what people have to say.

On the following pages are outlined a number of ways to communicate. The points below apply both to *explaining yourself* and to *bringing about change.*

Before your communications work group starts any year-round public communication program, ask yourself four questions:

WHAT single idea are you trying to put across to the community? It should be well thought out and built on the image needs of your group.

WHY are you mounting a community campaign? What is the goal: public education, membership, money, volunteers, legislative change, expansion of service?

WHEN will your campaign run? If you are looking for free time and space, avoid the heavy advertising months of November, December and January. Recommended are the months April through August — but try not to miss the vacationers.

WHO are you trying to reach? What part of the community: opinion leaders, women or men, business people, families with children, people within your group? Know your target audience before you develop the campaign and then design it specifically for them.

Good Reading

Scott M. Cutlip and Allen H. Center. *Effective Public Relations.* Englewood Cliffs, N.J.: Prentice-Hall Inc. Although geared primarily to corporations, the princples are sound for all groups.

Clearing the Air: Public to Public Communication Through the Mass Media. A handbook for citizens on how to make effective use of media facilities. Free. Write to Prof. Goldsen, Department of Sociology, Cornell University, Ithaca, New York 14850.

William Lawrence Rivers, *The Mass Media: Reporting, Writing and Editing.* New York: Harper and Row, 1964. A good journalist's guide for just about anyone.

Publicity and Public Relations - Notes for Community Leaders. Ontario Ministry of Culture and Recreation, Queen's Park, Toronto, Ontario.

Publicity Handbook. The Sperry and Hutchinson Company, P.O. Box 935, Fort Worth, Texas, 76101, 1972. (25¢)

Sallie E. Bright. *Public Relations Programs — How to Plan Them.* National Public Relations Council, 419 Park Avenue South, New York. N.Y. 10016.

Organizing your communications work group

1. Set up your budget. Be realistic. Work with what you have. Don't exceed your resources. A windfall to bail you out will rarely happen!
2. Where possible, seek out members for your work group from the media and the graphic arts — reporters, broadcasters, advertising specialists. Make sure whoever you involve is interested. Brief them thoroughly and give them the freedom to develop good material (within pre-set guidelines).
3. Remember, if you live in a rural area or small town, local branch offices can put you in touch with resources and experts at head office, to help with your campaign.

How to write a news release

> *The difference between the right word and the almost right word is the difference between lightning and the lightning bug.*
> Mark Twain

News forms the backbone of all communications programs. Persons, places and organizations are only of interest when something current is reported. It must be timely, informative, interesting and must affect the community. Human interest and personal recognition stories, the entire spectrum of human activities, the good things of life, children, nature, ecology are readable copy. (Copy is the word used by the media to describe the text of a story or announcement.)

Some local newsworthy items are:
- appointments to senior volunteer and staff positions;
- recognition of anniversaries and exemplary service;
- co-operation wih other organizations;
- predictions;
- hitching a local news aspect onto a national story;
- announcing new projects;
- health stories (these enjoy high public interest);
- task forces formed for specific purposes;
- conflict stories.

A few simple rules will make sure your releases are used:

The lead	Who, what, when, where, why and how are included in the first two paragraphs. The first sentence should contain an eye-catching fact or the news point of the story. A good lead catches the attention of a reader or listener.
The inverted pyramid	Each successive paragraph (from top to bottom) should be less significant than the one before it. News releases are cut from the bottom up.

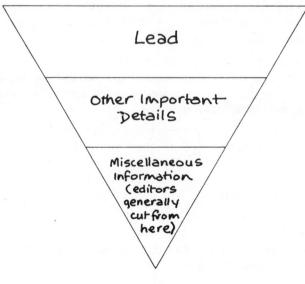

Keep it simple   Everyday words arranged in short, vivid sentences make a more lasting impression than a fancy literary style. Don't use jargon or technical language. When you have finished the draft of your press release, go over it and cross out any unnecessary words.

Be brief   The shorter your release, the better its chances of being printed or broadcast. Two sentences make a good paragraph in a press release. Almost every release can fit onto two double-spaced typewritten pages — which fills about 12 inches of a newspaper column. This is more space than most editors can give one item.

Ask yourself — if I weren't a member of my group, would this news interest me? If your answer is no, tear it up, If yes, you are ready to type your news release.

Use double-spaced typing on good quality, standard size (8½ x 11 inch) paper. Leave wide margins so editors can write changes. Place your group's name, address and telephone number in the top left hand corner of each page. Place the name, address and telephone number of a person editors can contact to find out more information, in the bottom left hand corner. In the top right hand corner, give the exact date of your news release. Say "For Immediate Release" — this means the editor can use it at once. Below the last sentence, type the number " - 30 - " in centre page. This shows your release has ended.

In addition to the above follow these suggestions for a successful news release:

1. Check every point of your release for accuracy — dates, names, facts, etc. The news media usually are blamed for inaccuracies when they happen. Don't damage your relationship with an editor by giving faulty information.

2. If you need numerous copies, mimeograph or photocopy them. This lets the editor know that others are getting the same release, and he can rewrite the lead. However, it is always better to carefully tailor a separate release to the editorial style of each newspaper, radio station, television station, business publication, etc.

3. Cultivate the acquaintance of people in the news media. An editor or journalist who is kept up to date with your organization's aims and programs can stand you in good stead, particularly when a controversial issue emerges.

144

Good Reading

Management and Fund Raising Centre. "News Release Checklist," 1977. One of a series of how-to pamphlets, "Organizing Your Way to Dollars." $1.50 each. Can be ordered from the Centre at 287 MacPherson Avenue, Toronto, Ontario M4V 1A4.

The news conference

Whatever is clearly expressed
is well wrote.
Lady Mary Wortley Montague

One of the most effective devices to get a story moving is a news conference. These must be planned and executed with care. A news conference includes *all* media. Call a news conference when:
- the story is very important;
- there are too many important facts about an important story to include in a news release;
- you have an important person to introduce, or a prestigious or unusual source of support for a project.

Being prepared is the key to good news conferences. News kits, consisting of fact sheets, statements, copies of speeches and reports, photographs, blueprints and plans — all applicable documents — should be available in advance. If possible, make sure a friendly media person gets things rolling with a "planted" question. To help television camera people, try to have on hand demonstration exhibits, scale models, charts or other graphics. News people are busy people — if you can state your message in fifteen minutes, don't take an hour!

Timing or scheduling is important. Whenever possible, hold your news conference during the working week. Pick a time least likely to conflict with any other event. Also think of the deadlines the media must work to. For example, a morning and an evening newspaper have quite different deadlines, and you'll need to decide where you most want coverage of your event.

Make sure you send a short written invitation to the media. It must stimulate interest, provide the basic facts and a name and telephone number to contact for more information. Attach a news kit or fact sheet and send by mail or messenger. Do not, if at all possible, use the telephone — a telephone message is easily lost. However, use the phone to follow up the invitations.

This checklist will help you:
1. Is a news conference necessary?

2. Are there other major events conflicting with the scheduling?
3. Are your sources of information ready for the news conference?
4. Have you briefed your spokesperson completely?
5. Are there other, more objective outsiders who can also appear at the news conference on your behalf?
6. What about physical arrangements: reserved seats, electrical outlets, space for TV cameras, a public address system, lighting control, etc.?
7. What about models, projectors, slides, cassettes and tapes, charts, pencils and pads? Any equipment operators must be trained in advance.
8. Will a stenographer and office equipment be available for people who are a long way from their offices?
9. Will the important spokesperson be available later for an interview.

A yearly news conference to outline your progress during the previous year and preview your goals and programs for the following year is a good way to keep the media and the public informed about your group.

The schedule should be displayed on a flip chart and printed in your magazine or other appropriate publication. This should be enclosed in the press kits.

Everything you have to say should be written in press release form. Meet those who didn't attend later and deliver your preview press kit.

Use your progress chart to plan a series of approaches to local media for interviews throughout the year, covering one or all of your programs. Each person on your communications work group should be responsible for contacting a set number of media people.

For an example of the *yearly schedule brochure,* contact:
The National Association for Mental Health, Inc., 1975 Agenda,
1800 North Kent Street, Arlington, Virginia 22209.

Official recognition

A week declared by a municipal or state official as your group's week (e.g., UNICEF Week) will give official status and recognition to your work. The office of a local mayor or your state's governor (if you are a statewide group) should be approached. Have an informal telephone conversation with an official located in the office to find out how this proclamation (for mayors) or similar procedure (for others) is normally carried out. Then apply officially in writing.

Obtain space in your local press, and publish an official proclamation or letter of support. Usually the government which makes the proclamation will pay the costs.

Good Reading

Telling Your Story. The National Center for Voluntary Action, 1785 Massachussetts Avenue N.W., Washington, D.C.

Facts about printing

One of the essential parts of a nonprofit group's life is printing. Information on this subject is difficult to find and sometimes hard to understand. Because of this, we have included this in-depth section to help you save money in the future.

Working with a printer

Many of us are intimidated by the printing process, and don't ask printers questions about how to reduce printing costs. As a result, we spend more than we need to.

The first step in dealing with a printer is to explain exactly what you want. You need to know four things in deciding how to produce any publication:

1. *Purpose.* Who will read it? What message will it convey? Will it be kept by the user or passed along?
2. *Quantity.* What is your real distribution requirement (not your best wish for the piece, but what you can distribute effectively)? Will your publication be the final form of information you wish to release? Would several printings over a period of time, in smaller quantities with revision to content or style, be more effective?
3. *Budget.* Is the money alloted enough for the job required? Would it be best to lower or raise expectations to suit the available budget or adjust your budget to suit the expectation of the piece? Is the money truly available? (Printers *must* be paid.)
4. *Time.* You must allow your printer enough time to manufacture printed products. When you shorten time for the printer, you should expect lower quality, more errors and higher costs

An investment in knowledge always
pays the best interest.
Benjamin Franklin

For information on printing we are indebted to Bob Levant, The Cumberland Press, 1266 Bay Street, Toronto, Ontario M5R 2B1.

Printing processes

Letterpress is the traditional method of printing. A raised surface consisting of metal type and engravings (of photographs, artwork, etc.) is inked, and paper is pressed against it. Letterpress requires expensive typesetting, and separate handling of type and engravings (also costly to make).

Most printing today is done by *offset lithography*. This process uses a single-surfaced plate, made by photographing a camera-ready layout. This layout may be a page proof of set type or may be typewritten. The plate (metal or cardboard) is inked and dampened with water, so ink adheres only to the image (the princple being that water and greasy ink don't mix). The image is printed first onto a

148

cylindrical rubber blanket and then rolled onto the paper. There are small offset presses (such as A.B. Dick and Multilith) as well as large ones. Some presses print two sides of a page at once. Others print several colours at once. Instant printing shops specialize in inexpensive, fast offset work: black printing on standard-sized (8½ x 11 or 8½ x 14 inches) white paper.

Mimeograph machines operate by forcing ink through a stencil onto paper. *Silk screening* works the same way. It is expensive for more than a one or two hundred copies, and it lacks the fine detail of other processes (thus it shouldn't be used for texts). Its advantage is it can deposit ink in a very thick film, making it possible to print light colours over dark colours. It also can print on a very wide range of surfaces. Colour posters usually are made by silk screening.

Photogravure uses a plate in which the image is etched into the metal. These presses are large and very fast, and are used for long runs (many copies), full-colour magazines, packaging, etc. The process renders colours faithfully.

Photocopying is a fairly expensive but quick method of reproducing camera-ready material. There are wet and dry photocopiers. The wet type uses a special coated paper that may feel unpleasant to touch. Generally, the quality of photocopies is low. Don't use a machine that produces copies with spots or dark patches. Photocopy shops may offer a selection of coloured papers. Recently, colour photocopying has been introduced, but it is very expensive.

Materials
Paper may be the single largest expense for your printing job. Paper is made of vegetable fiber (usually wood) and rags. The higher the rag content, the stronger and more beautiful the paper, and the more it costs. Currency is printed on high-grade rag paper. Newsprint is made from wood pulp.

Paper comes from the mill in a variety of standard-size sheets. Your publication should be of a size that will cut economically out of these sheets (with as little wastage as possible).

Paper is divided into grades (book, bond, cover, news, poster, wrapping, etc.) and weights. Weight is based on how much 1000 sheets of a standard mill size weigh. For example, bond paper in a 17 x 22 inch sheet size (from which two 8½ x 11 inch pages can be cut) comes in 16, 20 and 24 lb. weights. Changing to a lighter weight paper may make a difference in your postage costs later on, if you will be mailing large quantities of your publication.

Guide to printing

COMMON PROCESSES	QUANTITY	QUALITY	COST
Xerographic Copying (Photocopying)	short runs to 100 copies only	lowest available: what you see is what you get	you pay per copy
Offset Duplicating	200 to several thousand	better than the above	very low (standard sizes reduce start-up costs)
Small Press Short-run Printing	any quantity	good quality available from reputable printer	time & material (the simpler, the cheaper)
Sheet-fed Photo Offset	generally high quantity but discuss with printer	as good as you may need	time & materials
Web or Roll-fed Printing	volume printing; newspapers, etc., minimum 2000.	from newspaper quality to publishing quality	very low if sufficient volume
Silk Screening	short runs to 1,000	large solids bold colours	reasonable for poster work, packaging, or fabric printing
Letterpress	any quantity	printing and special purposes, numbering, imprinting, per-forating, cutting	time & materials
Other	Other processes are available for special needs. Ask your printer.		

OPERATOR	SHEET SIZE	AVAILABILITY AND AFFORDABILITY OF EQUIPMENT	SOME APPLICATIONS
unskilled operator, factory-trained service person	8½" x 11" 8½" x 14" or similar	equipment can be leased; copy cost is metered, with monthly minimum	reports ⎫ bulletins ⎬ to 25 copies
slightly skilled operator, factory-trained service person	8½" x 11" 8½" x 14" max. 11"x 17" min. 4" x 5" (approx. info.)	can be an in-house operation, costs $4,000 to $10,000 to set up	newsletters, pamphlets, multiple-page reports to several thousand copies
skilled	min. 4" x 5" max.19"x 25" all approx.	same as the above: cost can be included in the above with a slight additional investment (main difference is the use of better plate material)	stationery, posters, custom printing
highly skilled craftsman	general 25" x 38"	too costly for most organizations unless purchases are in excess of 1000 hrs. of presswork per year	book publishing, large-run stationery, precision full-colour printing, large areas of colour posters
skilled tradesman	to suit your needs	too costly to own	newspapers, books, catalogues, etc.
artisan, craftsman or tradesman	size of facilities dictates	if you have the space this need not cost $1,000	posters, prints on different surfaces: fabric, paper, plastic, metal, glass
skilled tradesman	any size	too costly	tickets, cards, posters, finishing offset sheets

Coated paper, used for printing photographs (particularly with letterpress) has a hard, smooth clay finish. It costs more than uncoated paper.

Using coloured paper is an inexpensive way of adding colour to your publication. Coloured paper costs a bit more, but not as much as full-colour reproductions.

Ink usually isn't a major expense. Coloured ink, another way of brightening your publication, is best used straight from the tin, mixing ink costs more. A light ink, such as yellow, is hard to read on white paper. Because printing inks are relatively translucent, you can't print a light ink on a dark background (except in silk screening). Also, ink changes colour when printed on coloured paper. Check beforehand to see if you like the result. Your printer should be able to show you sample books of paper and ink.

The surface of a paper that becomes too wet during printing (or whose fibers are easily lifted) may tear. Ink may show through from the other side on too thin paper. Ink troubles during printing may create mists of drops, mottling in solid areas, fuzzy letters, dense photographs. Don't accept copies with these faults.

Some circumstantial evidence is very strong,
as when you find a trout in the milk.
Thoreau

Photographs

One or two good photographs can liven up your publication. Be sure to use glossy prints in good focus. Poor photographs (cracked, faded, over-or under-exposed) can be improved by a retouch artist, but this may be expensive.

Printing presses cannot reproduce a photograph's continuous shadings. They can print a pattern of fine dots of varyng sizes, which gives the appearance of shading. Your photograph must be made into a *halftone* to break it up into dots. This is done by shooting the picture through an acetate screen that has a pattern of dots in its surface. The finer the screen (the more dots per inch), the finer the shading will appear in the halftone. Newspapers use 65-line halftones (very coarse). Magazines use a 120-line screen. Books may use a 133- or 150-line screen.

The more intricate the detail in your photograph, the harder it is to reproduce as a halftone (the detail gets lost). Photographs that already have been printed (in newspapers, etc.) must be re-screened, because the dots have been muddied by the paper and ink.

If you have several photographs to be made into halftones, try to have them worked on all together. This costs less than having a separate negative made of each.

Never write on the back of a photograph. The writing may show through. Don't fasten photographs together with paperclips, or roll them.

Colour transparencies (slides) can be reproduced, but certain colours may be lost (see the next section). Also, remember that ink on paper will not match the brilliance of light shining through film.

Photographs, drawings, etc. are given to the printer at your own risk. If they are valuable, have them insured privately.

How colour is printed

Full colour is obtained by printing the three primary colours (red, yellow and blue) and black together. The primary colours form secondary colours (orange, green, purple), and secondary colours mixed together form other colours. With colour halftones, instead of the ink actually being mixed to produce green, for example, dots of blue and yellow are printed side by side, giving the effect of green.

To separate the colours in your original, a camera operator makes a negative for each colour, using colour filters on the camera lens. Then, a plate is made for each colour and the paper is run through the press four times, until all the colours are added. This is called *four-colour process work*. Making *colour separations* (negatives) is very expensive, and takes more time than other halftone work, because the colour balance must be carefully maintained.

In general, colour adds considerably to your cost. Even if you are simply printing two colours of ink, in separate areas, a negative and plate must be made for each colour (black counts as a colour).

Natural coloured photographs and slides are easier to reproduce than colour drawings or paintings. To render delicate colours exactly, five-or ten-colour process work may be needed.

Most printers go by the custom that a reasonable variation in colour between colour proofs and the completed job is acceptable. *Make sure your colour proofs are printed on the same paper your publication will be printed on.*

> *The only certainty is that nothing is certain.*
> Pliny the Elder

Estimates and specifications

Ask several printers for written estimates (quotes) of the cost of printing your publication. Beware of too low estimates — you get what you pay for! However, some printers may have the equipment to handle your job more inexpensively. If possible, it is better to use a printer located near you.

To ask for estimates, you need to provide specifications. *Always submit the same specifications to various printers, so you can compare prices accurately.* The following information should be included:

- general description of your publication;
- measured size and number of pages;
- quantity desired (you can give more than one figure to get varying estimates.) Remember, it costs more to reprint than to have more copies printed in the first place.
- copy writing, copy editing, artwork or layout needed (a printer may have staff to do this, or send the work out);
- use of colour;
- paper stock (trade name and weight, or include a sample of paper you'd like);
- number of halftones needed, and any reduction or enlargement needed;
- number of colour separations needed — specify two-colour, three-colour or four-colour;
- typesetting needed (include the different sizes and styles you'd like). If your material is more than a few lines, include a copy so the printer can estimate length;
- binding, folding and any other finishing needed;
- the date you want your publication delivered.

If a printer prepares rough layouts, artwork, etc. and submits them with his estimate, you will be charged for this work.

Ask the printer to justify all costs, item by item. You're buying a custom-made object that you won't see until it's finished. Ask if you can save money by changing your layout, using lower quality materials, a different printing process, etc.

> *A foolish consistency is the hobgoblin*
> *of little minds.*
> Ralph Waldo Emerson

Watch out for minimum charges. For example, all halftone negatives up to a certain size may be charged a minimum figure, any typesetting (even two words) may be charged a minimum rate, or perhaps you will pay for a minimum quantity of paper even if it isn't all used for your job. You can get around these fixed costs by combining two or more publications and having them printed as one job.

Because of spoilage printers are permitted to charge for overruns (approximately 10 percent more copies are produced) to ensure that the original number requested is met. You can specify no overruns but you may in fact receive less than the original amount requested due to spoilage.

In some states you may not have to pay sales tax on the costs of publishing educational material. Check with the retail sales tax division of your government. Even if your publication is already printed, the tax may be refunded.

Proofs

A proof is a sample copy. Checking over proofs is your opportunity to see that everything is as it should be. Proofs can be made at several stages of the printing process. Some proofs "come with the job." Others you must pay extra for.

It is easier (thus less expensive) to make changes earlier rather than later in the preparation of your publication. The main cause of unexpected extra printing costs is author's changes. Make sure your material is in order before you give it to the printer.

When you have returned the proof, signed and marked "OK" or "OK with corrections," the printer is not responsible for correcting errors you missed.

The layout

A *layout* is a design or plan of how your publication will look. *Rough layouts* (sketches) help you and your printer decide on a final design. *Camera-ready layouts* are the finished product, ready to be photographed and made into a plate for printing.

It is easy to prepare your own camera-ready layout for simple publications. It also is less expensive than having a commercial artist or your printer do it for you. In general, the more work you do yourself, the less you need to pay your printer.

The first two references listed below explain how to prepare a camera-ready layout (typing your text, using transfer lettering for headings, choosing illustrations, etc.).

Good Reading

Management and Fund Raising Centre. "Know Your Printing and Save Money (Parts 1 and 2)" 1977. One of a series of how-to pamphlets, "Organizing Your Way to Dollars." $1.50 each. Can be ordered from the Centre at 287 MacPherson Avenue, Toronto, Ontario M4V 1A4.

Edmund J. Gross. *101 Ways to Save Money On All Your Printing.* Halls of Ivy Press, Suite 209, 10523 Burbank Blvd., North Hollywood, California, 91601, 1971. An excellent book, dealing with all aspects of preparing and printing a publication. Topics covered include:
- the camera-ready layout;
- choosing the right kind of artwork;
- getting more out of your photographs;
- selecting the best typeface;
- the many uses of photostats and negatives;
- paste-up ideas to save you money;
- paper grades, weights, sizes, colours and finishes;
- the need for proofs;
- bindery shortcuts;
- printing terminology (a superb glossary).

Clifford Burke. *Printing It.* Berkeley, California: Wingbow Press, 1972. (Widely available in paperback.) A printer's experiences and detailed instructions on preparing camera-ready layouts, and on setting up your own small press.

Eric K. Bain. *Display Typography.* London and New York: Focal Press Limited, 1970. A very good book on type and general principles of design, with sections on colour, photography, paper, printing processes and cost effectiveness.

Henry A. Paulsen. *A Course in Estimating.* Printing Industries of America, Inc., Washington, D.C., 1953. A training manual for printing estimators which covers just about everything about printing, in a detailed but readable way.

The Printed Word. Ontario Ministry of Culture and Recreation, Queen's Park, Toronto, Ontario. A general guide to planning and producing your publications.

Monthly magazine or newsletter

*The Public is merely
a multiplied "me."*
Mark Twain

This is an important update and cultivation tool. Those members of your communications work group with editing, writing and layout skills can do this effectively. If printing costs are high, publish every other month or even quarterly. However, don't shy away from a well-hand-written single sheet leaflet duplicated by an instant print process which involves a cardboard duplicating plate on an offset press (1978 price, $8.50 for 500 sides).

Constantly check and update your mailing list. Make sure your publication is getting to:

- all those in your community who will benefit from knowing about your group,
- all those who may be able to help you — now or in the future.

Monthly bulletin

Journalism is literature in a hurry.
Matthew Arnold

Assemble information in a concise form on each subject area — not more than four sentences per subject, followed by a name and phone number for more information. The bulletin could be used to fill the monthly gap if a more comprehensive magazine is published quarterly. A duplication system such as photocopying should be adequate to print a monthly bulletin.

Pamphlets and booklets

Many a writer seems to think he is never profound except when he can't understand his own meaning.
George D. Prentice

Many organizations publish pamphlets and booklets to help citizens use certain services or to teach ways of taking part in local community decision making. These should be well-prepared, concise, and easy-to-read without jargon or long words. Use diagrams and photographs or illustrations wherever possible. An advertising agency, a printer, an art school or a local paper can help with the design and printing.

Before beginning the project, think, "For whom?" Make sure it will reach them! Do you have a system for this? A task force is the best means of getting the job done. Reconvene the task force after a year to evaluate the booklet's or pamphlet's use and impact.

Many booklets come to an early and ill-fated end. The reasons for this include:

157

- lack of planning;
- lack of pre-testing;
- lack of evaluating.

The following checkpoints should be used as a guide:

1. What's your aim?
   - stated in specifics?
   - everybody consulted?
   - related to reader wants?
   - stated as desired action?
   - written and approved?

2. Who's your reader?
   - age?
   - sex?
   - occupation?
   - cultural background?
   - education?
   - social status?

3. What does the reader think?
   - major attitudes?
   - conscious of need?
   - solution already seen?
   - current attitude?

4. How will it get to reader?
   - distribution plan?
   - mailing costs?
   - envelopes?
   - convenient size?
   - supply and demand?
   - publicity or ads?
   - sub-distributors?

5. Are your facts straight?
   - material accurate?
   - story complete?
   - references OK?
   - both sides told?
   - obsolescence considered?
   - any conflict with your group's program?

6. Are your suggestions workable?
   - physically possible?
   - welcome to reader?
   - financially possible?

7. Do you talk the reader's language?
   - readability?
   - professional jargon?
   - reader's limitations considered?
   - easy index or table of contents?
8. How will your booklet look?
   - first impression?
   - interesting pages?
   - headings?
   - illustrations, photographs?
9. Will the reader react as planned?
   - text tested?
   - fair reader sample?
   - reader get the point?
   - willing to act?
   - able to act?
10. What's your score?
   - evaluation plan?
   - tied to aims?
   - control group?
   - interviews?
   - valid questionnaire?
   - statistical data?
   - bound-in reply form?
   - results known to staff?

Good Reading

Ten Checkpoints for Better Booklets 1956. Council of National Organizations, of the Adult Education Association of the U.S.A., 303 Lexington Avenue, New York 16, New York.

Alexander L. Crosby, *Pamphlets That Pull.* National Public Relations, Council for Health and Welfare Services, 419 Park Avenue South, New York, N.Y. 10016.

Wava McCullough, *Practical Layout: From Ideas to Printed Page.* New York: Art-Books-For-All Publishing Co.

Publishing to sell

Some nonprofit organizations have found that reports, studies, etc. have commercial potential, and they would like to make them available to a wider general audience.

There are three courses of action available:

1. Make an agreement with a commercial publisher to publish and sell the book.
2. Produce the book yourself then make an arrangement with a commercial publisher to promote and distribute it.
3. Produce, market and distribute the book yourself.

Each of these has advantages and disadvantages. With the first the publisher assumes full editorial, production and marketing control, relieving you of the many headaches of self-publishing and providing expertise where needed. On the negative side, you may feel that you have lost control of the project, as many of the publisher's decisions may be against your wishes. To avoid this situation, have your contract with the publisher as complete as possible, specifying those areas in which your approval is required before further action is taken. Also, remember that with a commercially published book, you will only receive a percentage (royalty) of the sales and the rest will be retained by the publisher.

Some publishers will request that you turn over the rights to your publication in return for an advance and royalties. If this is acceptable to you, it may be a good idea to put in the contract that they must publish your book within a certain time period or the rights will revert back to you.

With the second arrangement, you retain control over the editorial and production aspects, while sparing yourself the problems of marketing and distribution. This is likely to be a beneficial situation for many groups, as it is extremely difficult to get a book into bookstores and on mass market racks if you are not tied in with a recognized distributor. If you feel you have the competence to produce the book yourself, and if you are able to negotiate a favourable agreement with a publisher or distribution agent, this method may be the best. Under your distribution agreement, you can specify that the publisher is responsible for promoting (publicizing) the book; they are more likely to have the media contacts and the expertise for this job than the smaller group.

Under the third course of action, your group will assume full responsibility for producing and marketing your book. This requires a wide range of skills, and an efficient system of reaching your audience to sell the book. You can hire freelance editorial and design help (a publisher is likely to have the names of such people) or you can do it yourself. You will need good advice on printing methods and costs, which the production manager of a publishing or printing company may supply free if you solicit their support. You will have to co- ordinate your own publicity, using the advice in this manual. The most difficult part may be the actual sale of the book—ordering, shipping, payment, etc. Make sure you know what you are getting into before you start.

Who needs jargon?

Telling the truth to people who
misunderstand you is generally
promoting a falsehood, isn't it?
A. Hope

Jargon is technical words characteristic of a particular profession or other group. Some examples of jargon are:
"interpersonal dynamics" = the way people get along with others
"response repertoire" = the number of ways a person can respond to a situation (psychological jargon)
"resolution conflict" = inability to make decisions (managerial jargon)
Whenever someone uses a term or phrase that you don't understand, ask him to explain it. Professionals working in the community have developed a dazzling verbal shorthand to express difficult and complex theories.

Jargon is exclusive. Everyone who understands it is "in" — those who don't are "out." Beware. People who use jargon may be insecure, or they may not really understand the situation. Jargon turns off an audience. Eliminate it from your publications and public relations pronouncements. Otherwise those whose support you are trying to attract may lose interest or feel as if they are being "put down" by your group.

That must be wonderful:
I don't understand it at all.
Moliere

Public speaking

First, tell 'em what you're goin' to tell 'em;
then tell 'em; then tell 'em what you've tole 'em.
Unknown

Effective speaking is simply persuasive conversation adapted to fit the occasion and the audience.

Every speech has an:
- introduction,
- body, and
- conclusion.

To construct the body of a speech, ask yourself these questions:
1. What is the subject of my speech?
2. What particular points (not more than four) do I want to bring out?
3. Are these points relevant to this audience?

Answer each question in as much detail as possible. If your audience is likely to disagree with you, present both sides of any argument. Your suggestions are more likely to be accepted if they are in harmony with the principles and loyalties of the group you are speaking to, and clearly affect their personal lives. Make sure nothing in your speech is offensive.

Then, assemble your material into concise and logical order. Your discussion of each point should lead naturally to the next. Avoid using jargon or other words your audience might not understand.

Based on the body, give your speech an introduction and a conclusion. Your introduction should tell what your speech is about and capture your audience's attention. Your conclusion might be a summary of what you've said, an anecdote to illustrate your main points, or a challenge to action (for which you've already suggested a way to do it).

Put your speech down for a while. Sleep on it, then refine the material by asking the questions, "Are these points relevant to this audience?"

Read and reread your speech. Commit it *almost* to memory (but *do* memorize the beginning and ending sentences). To help yourself, write the key elements on cards that can be read at arm's length. Number the cards, and remember to bring them!

Points to remember in giving your speech:
1. Careful preparation is the basis of good presentation.
2. When you are introduced, walk leisurely to where you will stand, and make some natural gesture, such as moving an object on the speaker's lectern. Look at your audience for a moment and take a few deep breaths. This will put both you and your listeners at ease.
3. Talk *to* your audience, not *at* them. In other words, keep your audience *with* you. Speaking in public is an extension of ordinary conversation.
4. Make sure your words are clearly spoken, your voice loud enough (don't be shy!) and your pitch varied according to what you are

saying. Speak a little more slowly than you would in ordinary conversation.

5. Be relaxed and comfortable — this is essential for you to breathe and speak easily. Stand up straight and use your diaphragm to force air into the lower part of your lungs. Move about a little and use your hands for emphasis.
6. Look at your audience. Choose a few people scattered throughout, or talk to the back rows, occasionally emphasizing an important statement by looking at the people directly in front of you.
7. Accept interruption graciously.
8. Use your own personality. *Be yourself.*

Get as much practice as possible. Read stories aloud to your family, or talk into a tape recorder. Learn to listen objectively and critically to every speaker you hear, particularly yourself.

Good Reading

Management and Fund Raising Centre. "Effective Public Speaking," 1977. One of a series of how-to pamphlets, "Organizing Your Way to Dollars." $1.50 each. Can be ordered from the Centre at 287 MacPherson Avenue, Toronto, Ontario M4V 1A4.

Patrick O. Marsh. *Persuasive Speaking: Theory, Models, Practice.* New York: Harper and Row, 1967.

Dwight L. Garner. *Idea to Delivery: A Handbook of Oral Communication.* Encino, California: Dickenson Publishing Company, 1973.

James J. Welsh. *The Speech Writing Guide: Professional Techniques for Regular and Occasional Speakers.* New York: Wiley, 1968.

> *No man would listen to you talk if he*
> *didn't know it was his turn next.*
> E.W. Howe

The logo

> *It is through symbols that man*
> *consciously or unconsciously*
> *lives, works and has his being.*
> Thomas Carlyle

The logo is a simple design which identifies your group. It appears on

163

all your publicity material, exhibits, letterhead and envelopes, etc. Every day the public is exposed to thousands of messages. Tightly budgeted community groups must compete to get their message across. Symbology has now become the art of helping organizations achieve a separate image, helping them "stand out from the crowd." A well-designed symbol knows no language barriers. It works as a powerful marketing force.*

Here are some examples:

Conklin Shows: Carnival rides

(showing the clown who represents the fun of the midway)

Open Circle Theatre (the three principals in a semicircle, which is an open circle, looking outward to involve others with their theatre)

Your logo and group's name can be placed on a local TV station's own station-identification sign between programs. To arouse interest, have a community logo competition sponsored by your local newspaper.

*The author wishes to thank Chris Yaneff, Ltd., 119 Isabella Street, Toronto, Ontario, for their help in preparing this section.

Letterhead

Your group should have its own letterhead (stationery): it's an accepted way of inspiring confidence in those who don't know a great deal about your group. Your letterhead should show your group's logo, name, address and telephone number, and the names (usually printed down the left side) of important and prestigious members of your board or policy-setting group. At the bottom of the page you can have a one-line statement of your philosophy or a one-line description of this year's most important program, or your group's slogan. Your letterhead should be attractive but not extravagant. Ideally, it should be typeset and printed professionally on a medium quality paper. Have envelopes with your logo and name on them.

If you can't afford printed letterhead, you can make your own. Use letraset (instant lettering) and make photocopies.

Another important first impression is the way your letters, etc. are typed. Cramped typeface, characters which don't print or are clogged, poor alignment, poor spacing and poor layout show a lack of care and, in some people's eyes, a lack of overall competence.

How to write letters

The letter, next to the telephone, is the most commonly used instrument for communicating outside of your group. Your letters should be interesting, direct and clearly worded. Letters that express your personality are more communicative than those that follow a schoolbook formula.

Good Reading

Patrick Monahan. *Writing Letters That Sell*. New York: Fairchild Publishers, Inc.

Rudolph Flesch. *The Art of Readable Writing with the Flesch Readability Formula*. New York: Harper & Row, 1974. This book is filled with examples of how and how not to write, and includes a "human interest" and "reading ease" formula.

Letters to the editor

I have made this letter longer than
usual because I lack the time to
make it shorter.
Blaise Pascal

One of the easiest and most effective ways to bring your point of view to the attention of the public is to write a letter to the editor of a newspaper.

Here are some tips:
- Keep the letter short and to the point.
- Don't appear to be representing your group unless you've been told you can by your policy-setting group.
- In a small town, drop your letter off personally. The editor may be prepared to write an editorial — ask!
- Try to get supporting letters mailed directly from other respected organizations and individuals.

Ghost features

The top person in your group should write at least two feature stories a year, on a current issue facing your community. Local press welcome well written and interesting opinion articles. If your top person isn't a competent or interesting writer, have a professional writer ghost-write the story under the name of your top person.

Editorials

Most articles a newspaper prints or the electronic media airs are supposed to be objective — devoid of their writer's opinions. However, the owners and chief editors of newspapers, radio and TV stations reserve space or time to voice their own opinions on issues of concern. These usually are called *editorials*. Work to get the owners and senior employees of media interested in your issue and encourage them to support your viewpoint in an editorial.

New theatre deserves full public support

One reason Toronto is the toast of North American cities is the strong cultural community we have here. Good theatres, art galleries, the Science Centre and Royal Ontario Museum, ballet companies, opera, a symphony orchestra and much more.

Other cities can build tall buildings. But a lively, stimulating cultural life is something special, something to be supported and encouraged. Support and encouragement are needed, in fact, now for an ambitious plan to create a new downtown theatre centre in an historic old courthouse building on Adelaide St. just east of Yonge St.

Last year Metro leased to three theatre groups — The Open Circle Theatre, the New Theatre and Le Theatre du P'tit Bonheur — the 125-year-old courthouse that was the scene of some of 19th century Toronto's grisliest murder trials and which once housed City Council as well.

The three theatre groups have banded together to form a non-profit organization, Adelaide Court-Cour Adelaide, that plans to renovate the entire building, from the stale dungeons in the basement to the airy chamber on the second floor. But it won't just be a set of theatres.

Several restaurants are to be built into the project to help underwrite the costs of operating the theatres. Noontime public affairs shows and school programs are planned to make sure it's very much a people building in the daytime.

It's an exciting prospect. One more reason Toronto should continue to be a great place in which to work and live — or to visit. But it also needs community support right now. The backers have canvassed about $1 million from different government agencies. They have invited bids from restaurants. Now they need about $500,000 more from the people of Toronto — corporations, unions and individuals — to cover other costs in restoring the building.

No one in the project — managers, actors and actresses, secretaries or prop men — will get rich from it. Indeed they'll probably make just enough to scrape by on. But for the people of Toronto life will be a whole lot richer if this bold plan succeeds.

EDITORIAL FROM THE TORONTO STAR

The public exhibit

> *People in general do not willingly*
> *read if they have anything else to*
> *amuse them.*
> Samuel Johnson

We mostly associate the exhibit with trade or agricultural shows, not with community groups. An exhibit is proof you exist. A highly portable display, used year-round, is the ideal exhibit.

In most communities there are events which will include displays by community groups. In addition, you should try to place your exhibit in shopping plazas, at exits of factories and office buildings — in fact, any place where a large number of people will see it.

167

A local company can help with design and materials. Large stores, TV prop departments can help you put together an attractive, inexpensive portable exhibit. Also consider a small display for store counters.

Whatever you do, keep your display simple and uncluttered. Also, use large photographs, drawings and diagrams wherever possible. Keep words to a minimum.

The film

When your work speaks for itself, don't interrupt.
Henry J. Kaiser

Film production is extremely expensive. Before you plunge into movie-making, check to see if a film about your issue already exists. Page 14 of this manual gives some sources of film loans. The *Blue Book of Audio-Visual Materials*, available at larger libraries, lists some 300 suppliers (loan, rental, purchase) of educational films and other audio-visual material.

Short films are as good, if not better, than long ones. Also, they are less expensive.

Be professional. A ten-minute film about your group can be produced by an advertising agency that has persuaded a film production company (to which the agency gives a lot of work) to do the work for free or at cost. A university which has a film course can assign a student to carry out the project as a term requirement — free to you.

The film always should subtly solicit volunteers or another resource from its audiences. In other words, the film should reveal:

- an area of need;
- what your group is doing to lessen the problem;
- what more you and others can do, and how you need to expand your group's efforts.

To estimate the viability of your film, consider these formulas:

1. Will your film be shown for three years to as many people each year as it costs in dollars to produce? (This should start you thinking of TV and perhaps movie house use for your "short.")
2. Can it generate measurable resources equal to, or more than, the film's production costs?

If either or both of these formulas hold up, make your film.

In addition, super eight film equipment will give you a large screen, can be edited, and may do the job ideally for local showing. Single system super eight cameras which record sound on film are now available.

Super 8 Equipment	*Approximate Cost*
Camera	$200 — $600
Projector	$100 — $450
Film: 3½ minute silent with processing	$5.00—$6.50
3½ minute sound with processing	$7.00—$8.50

Where to go for help

Universities, community colleges and high schools give courses in filmmaking, often on an extension basis. They can be approached for facilities, equipment, skills and instruction. In addition, many educational institutions have large holdings of films and other audio-visual material available for loan or rental.

Center for Understanding Media
66 Fifth Avenue
New York, New York 10011

This organization conducts a program called Filmmakers-in-the-Schools, co-ordinating educational media projects in 40 states. The Center publishes catalogues and a periodical, *Medialog*.

Consortium of University Film Centers
c/o Visual Aids Service
University of Illinois
1325 South Oak Street
Champaign, Illinois 61820

An association of over 200 colleges and university 16mm film rental services.

University Film Association
Department of Cinema Studies
New York University
New York, New York 10003

Publishes a bimonthly, *Digest*. An affiliate, the University Film Foundation (Iowa State University, Ames, Iowa 50011) has conducted a survey of university film production facilities across the U.S.

Film-makers' Cooperative
175 Lexington Avenue
New York, New York 10016

A nonprofit film rental library whose members are independent filmmakers from across the country. Catalogue issued.

Good Reading

James S. Watkins. *Who's Who in Audio-Visual Presentation.* United Business Publications, 750 Third Avenue, New York, New York 10017. Lists 400 producers of films, filmstrips, videotapes, etc.

Audio-Visual Marketplace. R.R. Bowker Company, 1180 Sixth Avenue, New York, New York 10036. Names, addresses and product lines of all producers, distributors and other sources of educational A-V materials. Also lists national professional and trade organizations concerned with A-V.

The Focal Encyclopedia of Film and Television Techniques. New York: Hastings House Publishers, Inc. A definitive reference.

Lenny Lipton. *Independent Filmmaking.* Western Book Service, P.O. Box 3975, Rincon Annex, San Francisco 94119, 1972. Down-to-earth; solid information.

Mark Nickolas and Gunther Hoos. *Handbook of Super 8 Production.* United Business Productions, 750 Third Avenue, New York, New York 10017.

The audio-visual and video shows

The slide or slide/sound show. Slides are probably the most effective yet cheapest way to produce an audio-visual presentation. Good slides can be taken with a wide variety of cameras, and these and slide projectors can be found easily. With a tape recorder and a tape-slide synchronizer, you can join a sound track to your slide show.

Equipment	Approximate Cost
Camera (35 millimetre)	$125 — $400
Film (36 exposures with processing)	$5.50—$7.50
Slide projector	$150

Audio. Tape recorders, especially cassette recorders, are useful for recording meetings, conferences, etc. The growth of community radio stations and the increasing availability of air time on commercial radio (FM radio in particular) for community groups makes it possible for your group to get your message across to the public this way. Recordings produced by a good quality cassette and microphone are acceptable for broadcast by most radio stations. With a splicer, your audio tape can be edited and re-arranged.

170

Equipment	Approximate Cost
Cassette tape recorder	$100 — $200
Microphone	$ 50 — $100
Audiotape (one-half hour cassete)	$2.50

Video. The use of video (shown on a TV screen) by community groups has become increasingly widespread in recent years. Portable video units (portapaks) are simple to operate and can record sound and pictures at the same time. Video equipment often is available for use by community groups through schools and community colleges. In some cities, there are community media organizations that train people in the use of audio-visual aids, including video, and that also lend equipment. Cable TV companies are required to make television facilities available to community groups that wish to produce television programming for broadcast over the community channel, and they may be willing to provide equipment training.

Equipment	Approximate Cost
Portapak	$1750—$2000
Videotape (one-half hour)	$17—$20

Good Reading
A.C. Lynn Zelmer. *Community Media Handbook.* Netuchen, N.J.: Scarecrow Press, Inc., 1973. A complete guide to community media basics — print, audio, video film and photography.

Rudy Bretz. *Handbook for Producing Educational and Public-Access Programs for Cable Television.* Educational Technology Publications, Englewood Cliffs, New Jersey 07632, 1976.

Richard Robinson. *Video Primer.* Kinks Books, 33 West 60th St., New York, N.Y., 1974. Handbook on equipment and production techniques for small format VTR.

The Access Workbook. Alternate Media Center, New York University School of the Arts, 144 Bleecker Street, New York, New York 10012. Volume 1 deals with FCC regulations covering Community Access TV and outlines strategies for access. Volume 2 is a teaching and using guide for portapaks.

Community Video Report, Box 21068, Washington, D.C. 20009. A quarterly newsletter ($4/year). Contents include articles on community organizing and program ideas, reports on cable conferences, and analyses of FCC policies.

Len Biegel and Aileen Lubin. *Mediability: A Guide for Non-Profits*. Taft Products, Inc., 1000 Vermont Avenue N.W., Washington, D.C. 20005, 1975.

The annual report

Active accountability (letting people know what you've been up to) is the cornerstone of public understanding and acceptance of your group. A well-designed, easy-to-read annual report is one of the best ways to do this.

Groups who don't see their annual report as important usually prepare reams of mimeographed pages, written so only a few insiders are able to read them.

Here are some guidelines to preparing an effective annual report:

1. Form an annual report task force at least ten weeks before the report must be finished, to allow for delays.
2. This task force should consist of:
   - one policy-level person, e.g., a board member;
   - one senior staff person (if you have staff);
   - one person professionally involved in the communications field, particularly the print medium;
   - one person who has solid connections with writers, designers and printers in your community, such as an advertising executive.
3. Collect a number of corporate and nonprofit annual reports to get an idea of the content, design, etc.
4. Decide on the content, theme(s) and organization. Write the report.
5. Use figures to back up program descriptions wherever possible. Use graphs, and diagrams too. Photographs are particularly effective in making your report appealing.
6. Present an annual report in synopsis form only if the main report is long or complicated. State where the readers can locate the full report and encourage them to do so.
7. Mail your annual report to:
   a) All politicians including local, county, state and federal representatives.
   b) All civil servants involved in any way with your group or area of involvement.
   c) Community groups — including service clubs, churches, neighbourhood associations, volunteer centers, self-help groups, etc.

d) Local industry and chambers of commerce.

e) Organizations involved with similar issues or programs elsewhere. Ask for their reports in return.

f) The press.

g) Lawyers — mark the bequest section in these copies.

h) Any other lists available.

i) Your membership!

8. Attach letters to each mailing highlighting parts of the report of special interest to each particular group of readers. State how, where and why they can help your organization. Extend to them an invitation to meet with you. For example, politicians, lawyers and civil servants might be able to help change a government bylaw or enact new legislation. Community groups and industry could supply volunteers or needed materials. Groups similar to yours might supply solutions to certain operating problems. The press can expose your activities to a wider public — ask them for a feature article to be written. Ideally, letters containing a specific request or an offer to meet should be followed within ten days by a phone call.

9. If possible, always take photographs of your program events throughout the year. Make sure the photographer understands that pictures for reproduction require slight overexposure. You may find other display uses for the photographs in addition to your annual report.

10. Keep the text of your report crisp. Do not be afraid of being constructively outspoken — it usually keeps the reader's attention and communicates more. Remember: jargon, complicated phrases, cliches and long words are no-nos!

Good Reading

Frances A. Koestler. *Creative Annual Reports — A Step by Step Guide.* National Public Relations Councils of Health and Welfare Services, Inc., 419 Park Avenue South, New York, N.Y. 10016.

Hans Zeisal. *Say It With Figures.* New York: Harper and Row, 1957. Chapters one and three are excellent guides to figures, tables, graphs, proper use of percentages, etc.

The annual meeting

*Would that my hand were as
swift as my tongue.*
Alfieri

At least three months in advance of your annual meeting, form a task force specifically to organize it.

Don't overlook the potential that your annual meeting has. It can involve the community directly and indirectly by way of local media, and inform the public about your group and issues of concern to you. Above all, never use your annual meeting as an administrative necessity (even though it is a legal requirement for an incorporated group).

Organize the meeting along the lines of a conference or teach-in. Invite the public to attend. Try to plan the meeting so that newsworthy items are discussed. At the conclusion, send out press releases to local media. If your meeting brings persons from other communities, work with them to send press releases direct from the annual meeting to their media.

Your annual meeting can be used to measure last year's progress and set the coming year's goals. This may be the time to announce your group's upcoming yearly schedule.

Section B: Bringing About Change

The media campaign

If your group wants to change or direct public opinion, it is best to have a media campaign. In other words, an intense exposure of your message over a short period of time, e.g., a week, will alert the public to your message and help your point to penetrate.

A media campaign is usually launched with a news conference. Following the week's campaign, schedule your efforts over the next twelve months or appropriate extended time period.

Ancillary media

The Japanese printed English words on toilet paper. The result? Women learned English sooner than men. Studies indicated this was because women use more toilet paper! Moral: If you want to reach people, use what *they* use.

Other examples of ancillary media are:

- T-shirts with a logo or message;
- pens;
- matchbooks;
- calendars;
- bumper stickers;
- bookmarks;
- lapel pins.

Watch costs. Use donated products whenever possible.

Billboards

> *The superior man understands what is*
> *right; the inferior man understands*
> *what will sell.*
> Confucius

A most effective way of making a point, especially in a small community, is to use billboards. The chances are you will have to pay the cost of preparing the sign. However, the Outdoor Advertising Association of America, with a membership of about 500 billboard owners, may be willing to distribute and display your sign for free, provided the space is not being used by paying advertisers. For more information, contact the Association at 652 Madison Avenue, New York, New York 10022.

Trigger films

The big disadvantage of making films is their enormous cost. Also if a film is too long it leaves no time for discussion. Similarly, a long film can change people willing to discuss your issue into a tired, passive audience!

The trigger film technique uses an inconclusive dramatic scene to expose the area of your concern. The film scene is three to five minutes long and deliberately leaves the audience hanging, thus triggering a discussion. The idea is to motivate people to explore and question problem areas and find their own answers.

For more information about trigger films, contact: The Addiction Research Foundation, 33 Russell Street, Toronto, Ontario.

Also, see the section on film and audio-visual and video shows in Section A of this chapter.

175

Community media

> *Television is now so desperately*
> *hungry for material that it is*
> *scraping the top of the barrel.*
> Gore Vidal

Community media include:
- cable TV community channels;
- community nonprofit radio stations;
- community-controlled newspapers.

These can be used on a weekly basis by your group. Each will welcome an in-depth or interpretive presentation. Local broadcasters or a media training school are excellent sources of donated production talent. Don't be slick, yet be professional and, above all, interesting. Better one good show a month than four boring ones.

A community-controlled nonprofit radio station might be an important plus in your community. Why not look into it? Also consider stimulating another group to start a community-controlled newspaper.

Everyone wants to be a star! Watch out! Before spending effort and perhaps money on these projects, check the impact they will make compared with other strategies.

Good Reading
Turn on! An Introduction to Community T.V. Ontario Ministry of Culture and Recreation, Sports and Recreation Bureau, Queen's Park, Toronto, Ontario. Gives an idea of the potential of the community channel, base production information and techniques applicable to the equipment most generally available.

Issues for Study in Cable Communications. Sloan Commission on Cable Communications, 105 Madison Avenue, New York, New York 10016. A concise discussion of four basic issues confronting the growth of cable: the form to be created, content, regulation and control, and transmission.

How to Put Out a Community Newspaper. Organizers Library Servies, SCEF, 3210 West Broadway, Louisville, Kentucky 40211. One of a series of how-to guides for organizers.

Newspaper column or radio series

A newspaper is a circulating library
with high blood pressure.
Arthur "Bugs" Baer

If your group is involved with an issue or problem that affects most people in your community, such as family life education, physical fitness or personal budget management, you can start a newspaper column or radio series.

Find a well-known person to write the column or narrate the series. Pay him a monthly honorarium. Present a sample to a local paper or radio station and ask them to publish it on a weekly basis. Make sure your group is mentioned at the end of the column or program as the originator or "in association with." The alternative is to find a writer who will contribute directly to local media. Again, put some visible tag line identifying your group at the end of the column or program.

Remember, this technique will only allow a discussion of general issues related to your own field of interest — it is not an ongoing advertising outlet for your group.

Corporate sponsorship for radio and TV time

The ideal voice for radio may be defined as
showing no substance, no sex, no owner and a
message of importance to every housewife.
Harry V. Wade

Convince a large corporation to donate an already paid "slot" and replace their commercial message with your announcement. (They can do this without expanding their existing budget.) If you obtain a series of donated slots, add a tag line to your announcement thanking the donor. Thus, the corporation receives public recognition for their contribution and the donated slot is tax deductible, too.

Public service announcement

Radio and TV broadcast (i.e. not cable) stations make free time available to community groups and other organizations for public service announcements. However, this free time is usually allocated haphazardly and not during peak viewing or listening time.

Your message can be produced using free contributions by professionals, or by recruiting university students studying media.

These additional tips may help you:

- Writing a technically correct announcement is not enough. Make it unusual in some way, so it stands out. Radio stations, particularly in large urban centres, receive hundred of public service announcements — yours can be easily lost in the shuffle. Also, present your public service announcement copy in person, and follow up with a phone call.
- Copy for television spots should be typed in ten-, thirty-, and sixty-second form. These should be supported by coloured film or slides to dramatise the copy.
- Word counts for "spots" are: 25- 30 words for 10 seconds
                                 40- 50 words for 20 seconds
                                 60- 70 words for 30 seconds
                                 130-140 words for 60 seconds

178

BE INTERESTING AND KEEP IT SIMPLE

- If slides are used, the maximum is: 3 slides for 10 seconds
                                         5 slides for 20 seconds
                                     12 slides for 60 seconds
  Less than the maximum is desirable.
- More than one set of "visuals" is required if there are to be several television showings in a day. Check with the station's program director.

See the information on audio-visual and video shows in Section A of this chapter about tape recording and slides.

To find out more, consult:

Television Commercials. Hastings House, Inc., 10 East 40th St., New York, N.Y. 10001. General information and listings of film and videotape production studios, ad agencies, etc.

Network Rates and Data. Standard Rate and Data Service, 5201 Old Orchard Rd., Skokie, Ill. 60076. Bimonthly, $8/year. Gives radio and TV network rates, discounts, production facilities, etc.

Influencing existing media programs

Most community groups are not capable of producing dramatic (fictional) media programs, which communicate issues to the public in an entertaining way. Yet there is an amazing impact to be had here. Look at the success of "All in the Family," with its perennial bigot Archie Bunker, as a vehicle for social interpretation.

If your group wants to make a point in this way, write an outline and mail it to the producers of a television or radio dramatic series. They are always looking for topical material which reflects real life concerns — especially for their situation comedies.

In addition, you can ask intelligent and creative media stars to develop socially concerned specials. Dick Cavett's one hour special, "V.D. Blues," successfully took a humorous tack with a serious health problem. Within minutes of the show's ending, health clinics were swamped with calls, which demonstrates the need to make follow-up arrangements to cope with public response. Finally, you can write to a TV or radio show host and ask them to mention your particular message at their show's closing.

This type of influencing is not unlike lobbying (see page 192). Try to get the support of other people, to write back-up letters or introduce you to the people who make decisions for radio and TV dramatic productions.

Poster competition

An especially creative and community-involving way of finding out how to get your message across is to have a poster competition. Ask local media to help you with this. A local newspaper, radio or TV station could organize the competition in two categories: professional and amateur.

The competition would invite local people to submit a slogan and a graphic design to either communicate what your group is about, or promote understanding of a problem or issue.

Advertising agencies, public relations companies, and artists would be aproached for the professional category; school children, university students and the general public for the amateur category.

The poster below resulted from a poster competition called the "Care Campaign," sponsored by the Toronto *Telegram* in 1971.

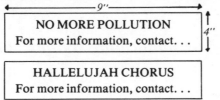

The three-word flash

The least expensive way of making a point to the general public is to print by offset duplicating a message of not more than three words.

NO MORE POLLUTION
For more information, contact. . .

HALLELUJAH CHORUS
For more information, contact. . .

Preferably, the printing should be in bold red letters on a white background.

Paste your "flashes" up all over — telephone poles, etc. Short messages of this nature can be read by both pedestrians and drivers.

How to use community theatre

*Radicalism: the conservatism of
tomorrow injected into the affairs
of today.*
Ambrose Bierce

With the upsurge of public interest in local theatre, this has become an exciting way to increase awareness of important issues in the community. Small professional theatre companies sometimes seek out local material for new plays. For example, Open Circle Theatre of Toronto has produced plays on lead pollution, attitudes of police toward the public and the destruction of residential areas. Contact them at 390 Dupont Street, Toronto, Ontario M5R 1V9 to find out more.

This type of theatre usually follows a documentary format. Here are the steps.

1. The issue is identified.
2. Professional actors interview and tape record persons involved with all sides of the issues.
3. The tapes are transcribed.
4. The transcriptions are edited.
5. The edited transcripts become the basic script.
6. The basic script is treated for dramatic interpretation, e.g., mime, dance, song, music, etc.

Some theatre companies will take their production to the communities, so the people affected by an issue can gain clearer understanding of their own predicament. Urge a theatre company to present your issue to the community. A good production can be adapted and used for television or radio, thus reaching a wider audience.

Section C: Communicating Within Your Group

Introduction

*My own business always bores me
to death; I prefer other people's.*
Oscar Wilde

182

Groups, no matter how small and intimate, have communications difficulties.

Simply expressed, put two people together, and there are misunderstandings. This fact, applied to the complex forms of organization that we create today, is both frightening and challenging. Effective internal communications are essential to the smooth functioning of any organization.

A breakdown of communication within a group usually heralds the breakdown of the group itself!

Board of directors (or policy-setting group)

To keep this group communicating within itself:
- Each person must have all the current addresses and phone numbers of the others.
- Any meeting of a sub-committee of the policy-setting group must circulate a written summary of their discussions for the full group to see.
- At least twice each year (more if possible), the policy-setting group should get together socially. Include staff.
- Meetings of the board must be recorded and this record (the minutes) circulated as widely as feasible. Don't alienate people within your group by keeping unnecessary secrets.

Board of directors (or policy-setting group) and staff

For best communications:
- Don't be a board room snob! Remember, the policy makers and staff must have a working partnership. Make sure *all* (including administrative support staff) are invited to attend every policy group

meeting. This invitation is only revoked when confidential matters dealing with staff are on the agenda.

- Make sure all staff receive minutes of all board meetings.
- All board members and staff should meet socially at least twice each year to better understand each other's activities and problems.
- Include staff at the policy group's orientation session.

Among staff

*When speculation has done its worst,
two plus two still equals four.*
Samuel Johnson

Staff should meet (for breakfast or another not-so-busy time) at the beginning of each week to:
- report on progress with their projects;
- share general information;
- file weekly schedules.

Take care not to allow these meetings, in spite of their importance, to infringe on the regular times of operation. If there is a lengthy matter left undiscussed, it should be dealt with the following morning or at a special meeting held at another time.

Staff might consider an informal weekly gathering for the purpose of keeping fit (yoga or mixed soccer, etc.) and for informal communication. No one in your group should be excluded from such a gathering — nor should anyone be forced into attending. This type of gathering also is an excellent way of communicating with other community groups.

Once each year, staff and volunteers should take a weekend away to review their work, learn new or improve existing techniques, and set plans for the coming year.

Phone-in bulletin

If your group or organization has branches spread over a large area, such as a city or state, it should have an information phone-in bulletin arrangement (see "The Network Bulletin," in Chapter 12).

Each branch must supply each month three- or four-sentence reports on each of its activities to be published in a newsletter. The name, address and phone number of the most knowledgeable person for each activity should be included at the end of each item.

Subject areas might be:
- new programs;
- staff changes;
- news of other organizations;
- government relations;
- helpful publications;
- new resources.

A volunteer in each branch can be the reporter to a head office volunteer editor.

For an example of a phone-in bulletin, contact the Toronto Youth Program Information Exchange (TYPIE), 357 College Street, Toronto, Ontario M5T 1S5.

Writing reports

Task forces, committees and individuals all are accountable (actively responsible) to other people within your group. One way of outlining your activities and showing your progress is to write a report.

Read the sections of this manual on "How to Write a Brief" in Chapter 6 and "Who Needs Jargon?" in this chapter.

Good Reading
Help! I Have to Write a Report. SEDFRE, 1 Penn Plaza, New York. 10001, 1971. A guide to successfully preparing and writing reports, formal and informal. Includes pointers on outlining the report, writing an interesting "lead," and ensuring an appealing appearance. There is a section on keys to good writing.

Petty politics

> *Suspicion always haunts the guilty mind.*
> William Shakespeare

At all times, remember that you need all your energies to achieve your basic program goals.

If you are working closely with other people, be patient with their idiosyncrasies — you have a few, too. If someone is truly undermining the group in some way, an appropriate person should talk to him in a friendly, direct way. Ask questions; don't accuse. Above all, don't engage in discussion about anybody behind his back. This leads to a breakdown of trust in the organization.

Play it straight and open!

> *Man is the only animal that*
> *laughs and weeps; for he is the*
> *only animal that is struck with*
> *the difference between what things*
> *are and what they ought to be.*
> William Hazlitt

11

Government relations work group

*Public Opinion is stronger than
the legislature, and nearly as strong
as the Ten Commandments.*
Charles Dudly Warner

The reasons for government relations

*It seems the less a statesman amounts to,
the more he loves the flag.*
Frank Hubbard

Citizen groups are always concerned about the impact government has on their community.

People in their communities can help or hinder government action at many strategic points. The process of influencing government is known as "public participation in (government) planning policy and programs."

The reasons why the ability to influence government is important are:*

1. People have more respect for those laws on which they have been consulted.
2. People identify strongly with programs they have helped plan.

* From the *Ad Hoc Report of Community Development Experts*, Economic and Social Council, United Nations, page 5.

3. People perform better in projects they have helped set up.
   Jean H. Legasse has summed up his observations as follows.
a) All persons or groups, no matter how unambitious they may appear on first encounter, have a strong desire to better their condition.
b) *If they have not* been able to noticeably improve their condition, it is because the difficulties which they would have to overcome to achieve this are bigger than the skills and resources at their disposal.
c) All persons or groups will take advantage of opportunities of improving their condition once it becomes evident to them that the skills and resources at their disposal are sufficient to enable them to improve their lot and they are allowed to do so on their own terms.
d) In order to create conditions conducive to (c) above, it is often necessary to influence several spheres of personal and community activities at once. Lack of change in one sphere could prevent change from occurring elsewhere.

The ongoing monitoring function

*Govern a great nation as you
would cook a small fish. Don't overdo it.*
Lao Tsu

Your government relations work group is responsible for monitoring, year-round, the activities of all governments which may affect your group and local community. This includes:
- municipal (local) government;
- county government;
- state government;
- federal government.

This monitoring function can be carried out in a number of ways:
1. Retired people or a service club can attend general and committee sessions of a government and report back to your group. These people also can meet with government employees and occasionally with politicians. (They must invite someone from the policy level of your group when meeting with politicians.)
2. Subscribe to the *Congressional Record* and the *Federal Register* (each $45 a year) to keep up with new laws and regulations.
3. Subscribe to the reports of debate in your state legislature.

4. At every opportunity, submit briefs to legislative committees and local government departments.
5. Meet regularly with politicians.
6. Know the information officers in departments related to the area in which your group is active. Put them on your mailing list, and ask to be put on theirs. This is one way of finding out about new funding programs and changes in legislation.
7. As your group establishes its presence, make sure you are in the running to sit on government advisory committees, etc.

The League of Women Voters, with 145,000 members and more than 1,300 local chapters, has shown how effective volunteer groups can be in monitoring government proceedings at every level. To learn more about the workings of this organization, write to the League of Women Voters, 1730 M Street N.W., Washington, D.C. 20036. Your local chapter of the League will share its findings with your group.

If you live in a country run by committee,
be on the committee.
Graham Summer

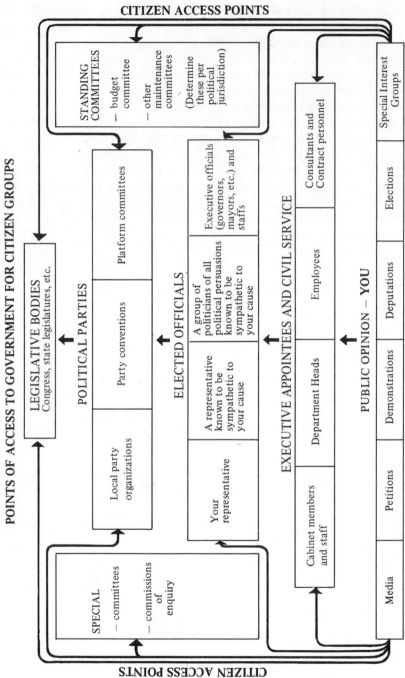

POINTS OF ACCESS TO GOVERNMENT FOR CITIZEN GROUPS

LEGISLATIVE BODIES
Congress, state legislatures, etc.

STANDING COMMITTEES
– budget committee
– other maintenance committees
(Determine these per political jurisdiction)

POLITICAL PARTIES

Local party organizations

Party conventions

Platform committees

SPECIAL
– committees
– commissions of enquiry

ELECTED OFFICIALS

Your representative

A representative known to be sympathetic to your cause

A group of politicians of all political persuasions known to be sympathetic to your cause

Executive officials (governors, mayors, etc.) and staffs

EXECUTIVE APPOINTEES AND CIVIL SERVICE

Cabinet members and staff

Department Heads

Employees

Consultants and Contract personnel

Special Interest Groups

PUBLIC OPINION – YOU

Media

Petitions

Demonstrations

Deputations

Elections

CITIZEN ACCESS POINTS

Steps toward change

Governments are beginning to encourage citizen input into their planning process. This trend, however, tends to favour the well-established organization over the newly-formed "grassroots" citizen group. It is up to new groups to rapidly build legitimization for themselves, by developing ongoing contact with government. Remember these points:

- *Don't go it alone.* You need the help of other groups and individuals when you approach government. Ultimately, you need the help of government to achieve change.
- *You have an obligation to inform and influence government.* To fulfil this obligation you must not overlook opportunities and existing channels (media) for comment and ideas.
- *If all constructive avenues of communication have failed,* consider a more agressive stance (see "Public Demonstrations and Symbolic Acts of Protest" in this chapter).
- *Establish credibility.* Make sure your target knows who you are, the reason for your concern, your goals, and the extent of your base in the community. Demonstrate your seriousness and the need for action. Put the department on your mailing list.
- *At first, suggest — don't demand.* This leads to better communication.
- *Obtain support within the specific department.* Don't ignore civil servants while wooing legislators.
- *Be realistic. Solutions are not easy.* See both sides, yet don't talk yourself out of your reason for influencing a government in the first place!

Here is a sample process to influence government policy.
1. Research and put together your case.
2. Determine the most effective points of access, and find out when these will be available for your presentation.
3. Get suport for your case from:
   — other organizations;
   — your membership;
   — the general public — letters to politicians, public demonstratons, etc. Use the media.
4. Meet with legislators or other politicians to present your case.
5. The next day, hold a 45-minute "legislative breakfast" for all political parties (or equivalent for municipal politicians). Present

your case while they eat their breakfast en route to the office. Charge for it!

6. Hold a press conference following the legislative breakfast.
7. Systematically meet with heads of pertinent departments over a follow-up period of three weeks.
8. Make plans to stay in touch.
9. If you have exhausted a responsible process of negotiation and have not received a satisfactory answer, take your case to the media.

If your group is geographically distant from the politicians you want to reach, place a conference call. The conversation can be amplified so that several people can participate. Check with your local Bell Telephone conference operator for specific details as to procedure and cost.

> *Arguments are extremely vulgar,*
> *for everyone in good society*
> *holds exactly the same opinion.*
> Oscar Wilde

The lobby

> *My experience with government is when things are*
> *non-controversial, beautifully co-ordinated*
> *and all the rest, it must be that there is*
> *not much going on.*
> J.F. Kennedy

A lobby is a well organized ongoing series of communications with all levels of government. Its aim is to persuade governments to start new policies, change existing ones, or increase government support (including dollars) for a program or group. This is called "influencing" government.

Remember that if you are seeking government funding, you should make your request before the money is needed. This allows time for the funds to be entered in the government's estimates.

Good Reading
Jeffrey M. Berry. *Lobbying for the People: The Political Behaviour of Public Interest Groups.* Princeton, New Jersey: Princeton University Press, 1977.

Carol Derfner. *Public Affairs Handbook.* The Grantsmanship Centre, 1015 West Olympic Blvd., Los Angeles, California, 90015.

Edgar Lane. *Lobbying and the Law: State Regulation of Lobbying.* Berkeley: University of California Press, 1964.

Know Your Community. Education Fund, League of Women voters, 1730 M Street N.W., Washington, D.C. 20036, 1972. A guide to learning about local government for community groups.

The National Directory of State Agencies. Information Resources Press, 2100 M Street N.W., Washington, D.C. 20037. An annual directory of departments and officials in all fifty states, listed both by state and by function.

State Offices of Community Affairs. Council of State Governments, Iron Works Pike, Lexington, Kentucky 40505. Describes the agencies and their functions.

Michael Barone, *et al. Almanac of American Politics.* New York: E.P. Dutton and Company. A state-by-state list of governors, senators and congressmen, with an analysis of each congressional district and a profile of the incumbent. This very useful book also provides voting statistics, examines voting trends, and lists congressional committees and their members.

Robert N. Kharash. *The Institutional Imperative: How to Understand the United States Government and Other Bulky Objects.* New York: Charterhouse Books, 1973.

United States Government Manual. Order from the Superintendent of Documents, U.S. Government Printing Office, Washington, D.C. 20402. The official handbook of the federal government. Begins with the text of the Constitution and goes on to describe the structure and activities of every branch, department and agency of the national government.

The O.M. Collective. *The Organizer's Manual.* New York: Bantam Books, Inc., 1971. Also provides information on staging acts of protest (see the following section).

Public demonstrations and symbolic acts of protest

Kites rise highest against the wind — not with it.
Winston Churchill

When all else has failed and you strongly believe in your position, you can use one of the following legal strategies:

- a public rally with speakers;
- a protest parade or march;
- an employee strike or work-to-rule;
- boycotts of certain products or services;
- a vigil;
- fasting as a protest;
- a sit-in and other forms of occupying an opponent's premises.

Before starting any of these tactics, thoroughly check the legalities of your plan and evaluate all personal risks and implications. Make sure that you have your facts right, are well organized, and make the media aware of your plans once (not before) they are underway.

3

Bits and Pieces

12

Bits and pieces

Turn competition into co-operation.

Chris Vicary

Pages 196 to 201 in this chapter describe how to get together with other groups to:
— co-ordinate activites;
— save dollars;
— strengthen programs and personnel;
— improve inter-organization communication.
   Other issues of interest to the nonprofit organization are discussed in the final pages.

Networking

Coming together is a beginning;
keeping together is progress;
working together is success.

Unknown

The diagram below shows how different groups working in the same field can plan and mobilize for action together. The network is an expansion of the coalition (see "The Coalition," Chapter 3 of this manual). Organizations participating in a network gain considerably from:
• regular sharing of current information;
• mutual support, e.g., sharing resources, ideas, etc.;

196

- joining in a common front should they need to make a collective statement.

Each participant's autonomy is protected to the full. Groups working in any field can use this highly successful model.

NETWORK

A broadly dispersed, mixed group of individuals representing groups, organizations and governments, who affect or work within the field of interest. The network receives information from and contributes to a bulletin. Its members are invited to information-sharing meetings.

INFORMATION-SHARING GROUP

A regular informal exchange of current information. Invitations to attend are sent to coalition and network members.

COALITION

A formally structured inter-organization planning and action group. Its members can be senior personnel elected from the information-sharing group.

Notes:

Staff: This proposed three-part system normally requires at least one full-time staff person to build and maintain it.

Financing: Individual coalition members should pay a membership fee of $1-$25 per year. Members representing groups should pay a larger fee, e.g., $1,000 per year, depending on ability to pay. All members of the information-sharing group and the network should pay a subscription to the bulletin plus a one-dollar charge per information meeting. Half of the three-part system's financing should come for its participants.

Good Reading

Seymour B. Sarason, *et al. Human Services and Resource Networks.*
San Francisco: Jossey Bass Publishers, Inc., 1977. This detailed study
describes the formation, growth and evolution of a human services
network that eventually involved private and public agencies and
hundreds of people in several states. The book also provides a general
analysis of the network concept, emphasizing such points as problems
of communication, the importance of network meetings, the role of
leadership, and the causes of failure of services networks.

H.W. Demore, Jr. and D. Harshbarger. *A Handbook for Human
Service Organizations.* New York: Behavioral Publications, 1974.

H. Turk. "Interorganizational Networks in Urban Society: Initial
Perspectives and Comparative Research." *American Sociological
Review,* 1970, no. 35, pp. 1-19.

J.K. Benson. "The Interorganizational Network as a Political
Economy." *Administrative Science Quarterly,* 1975, no. 20, pp.
229-249.

Malcolm Shookner. *Human Service Networks and Coalitions.*
Human Services Study Group, Goddard College, Plainfield, Vermont, 1976.

The network bulletin

*Understanding is always the understanding
of a smaller problem in relation to a
bigger problem.*
P.D. Ouspensky

The network shares information among its members through publication of a regular bulletin, say every other week.

The bulletin involves all groups and organizations working in the
same field. In addition, it keeps all those who can affect a particular
field of interest supplied with up-to-date information; e.g., politicians, governments, resource donors, recipient groups, other agencies,
etc.

The bulletin should cover such subjects as:
• new programs and groups in the community;
• new legislation and programs of government;

- new funding sources and up-dated reports on their recent support to groups;
- new publications, films and studies;
- staff changes within groups;
- staff vacancies;
- special events.

Write only three or four sentences per subject. Put special emphasis on where to locate more information at the end of each subject: a contact name, phone number and address.

The bulletin is a two-way information-sharing tool. Each reader is obliged to phone in information regularly in return for the information received. The more formalized the input process, the better; e.g., a designated reporter for each group, with a phone-in time.

Summaries of the information-sharing and coalition meetings, along with the names of those attending, should be attached to the bulletin. An invitation to the next information-sharing meeting should also be attached.

The community secretariat

The trouble with opportunity is that it always
comes disguised as hard work.
Herbert V. Prochnow

This is a centre of resources for citizen groups located in a particular area.

The secretariat should be located in a well-known and used community facility such as a library, shopping plaza, storefront or community centre. It should contain:
- duplicating machinery;
- an inventory of people and resources who/which can help citizen groups with a wide range of tasks; e.g., typists, bookkeepers, brief writers, lawyers and accountants;
- meeting space;
- consultation for all types of citizen groups.

Usually, one full-time staff person co-ordinates the secretariat. This person is responsible to a board of directors made up of community people and representatives of groups using the secretariat.

The secretariat must be careful not to become a "closed shop." On the other hand, it must not stretch its resources too thinly. It may have to say no to groups from time to time. Criteria must be developed for admission. All those using the centre must help find resources for the secretariat. Again, criteria should be developed to determine who should contribute what to the resource pool, and how.

For more information on the community secretariat, contact the Social Planning Council of Metropolitan Toronto, 185 Bloor Street East, Toronto, Ontario.

Sharing facilities

> Good binding requires no knots,
>   yet no one can loosen it.
>   Lao Tsu

Facilities are expensive and often beyond the finances of citizen groups, from both a purchase and maintenance point of view. A number of independent groups and organizations can use one building, sharing overall costs and responsibilities. This results in co-ordination of effort, collaboration on certain projects, and cost savings (certain administration and all building maintenance costs can be shared).

The following is an outline of a multi-service model which is being used currently for groups of social service agencies. The same principles can be used for other kinds of citizen groups.

A multi-service centre housing a group of agencies which serve family needs might include:

- counselling — marriage, individual, psychiatric;
- medical — doctors, public health nurses, a VD clinic, planned parenthood groups;
- big brothers and big sisters;
- legal aid (lawyer);
- psychiatric groups;
- youth groups, senior citizen groups;
- day care centre;
- budget advisor;
- municipal and state welfare offices;
- state employment office.

These groups use one administrative pool (except when professional ethics dictate more confidentiality) consisting of:

- an office manager;
- a bookkeeper;
- secretarial services.

People using the centre (clients) first meet an intake worker, for all the services. This worker interviews them and directs them to the ap-

200

propriate service. Member groups must be prepared to give up their identities as separate organizations and simply be regarded as centre services.

Each of the groups has a representative on the management committee, to cope with the technical problems of the centre. The centre is run by a co-ordinator who is responsible to the operations committee.

The multi-service centre ideally is controlled by a board of directors representing community concerns. This community board is professionally advised by the participating organizations via the centre's co-ordinator.

Sharing overhead (basic operating costs including facilities)

You won't skid if you stay in a rut.
Frank Hubbard

Even though your group may be housed in its own facility, you should always be on the lookout for opportunities to reduce your administrative costs by sharing them with other groups. For example, you can share the cost of office machinery, bookkeeping, secretarial services or public relations staff. Staff are generally more portable and easier to share than equipment.

Use a network bulletin or write a form letter to other groups you know and think you can work with.

Your group should consider locating in the same building as another similar group. This is not a multi-service centre since it does not involve a single board of directors.

Systematically check through all your operations and equipment needs and seek shared arrangements wherever possible. Funding sources are impressed by this type of cost savings effort.

For information about a similar arrangement involving three theatre companies under one roof, contact Adelaide Court/Cour Adelaide, 57 Adelaide Street East, Toronto, Ontario.

How to use consultants

*Fashions have done more harm
than revolutions.*
Victor Hugo

The cliche putdown of the consultant is that, to tell you the time, the consultant will borrow your wristwatch, tell you the time, and then sell the watch back to you.

The moral of this quote is, quite simply, that *you* probably have the answers to your own problems, so why pay money to hire someone else to give you the same answers?

There are some advantages to hiring a consultant:
1. Strategically, the consultant is regarded as a neutral person and therefore is able to make objective and unbiased recommendations.
2. Persons often will speak more freely to an outside consultant than to someone from within your group.
3. The consultant possesses specialized skills of observation, analysis and organization.
4. The consultant has the time to search and probe.
5. A consultant is not personally involved with people in your group. He is less likely to be swayed by personalities in his search for the best way to run your organization.

There are also some reasons to be wary:
1. A consultant can cost a lot of money. Check with other groups to get an idea of price.
2. Many recommendations can be put forward, but these are useless if your group does not have the people or resources to put them into practice.
3. Many consultants are business-oriented and cannot understand the different techniques used by community groups. Check their experience with community groups before you hire them. Ask for copies of reports, manuals, work plans, etc. from other jobs they have done. If practical hire a consultant for a few days without committing your organization to a long-term contract. This will permit you to determine if the consultant is going to meet your needs.
4. Know what you want:
- someone to evaluate the effect of your program?
- someone to evaluate the efficiency of your group from a management perspective?

While the two are intricately linked, they *may* require two people with different skills.

5. In order to save time and money and insure success, be prepared. Provide your consultant with all the internal information he requires.

6. The areas a consultant should look at are those outlined in Chapter 5 on planning and evaluation. Before you engage a consultant, ask in an interview what he knows about the points suggested for evaluation. Also ask for a written outline of the consultant's code of ethics and expectations of you, a projected timetable, reporting procedures, number of man-days and/or a description of the end results, and last but not least who's doing what. Ask for references and, if possible, copies of his work for other community organizations.

7. It is better to carry out your own evaluation using the consultant to help design questionnaires and provide you with methods to aid the process. The consultant can be an observer to your evaluation and file an independent report.

Remember, a local corporation, management consulting firm, university school of business, or government office may be able to lend you, free of charge, personnel with management and program evaluation skills. Phone or submit written requests for this service (see Chapter 6 of this manual).

Good Reading
Voluntary Action Leadership, Spring 1977. National Council of Voluntary Associations, 1214 16th Street N.W., Washington, D.C. 20036. "Using Consultants — A Guide for Administrators," pages 18-22.

Building a facility and choosing an architect

Events are not affected, they develop.
Sri Aurobindo

It is generally easier to raise funds for new facilities. To those not experienced in funding community groups, bricks and mortar are tangible evidence of exactly how their funds are being spent.

The following should help your group with the first steps of creating a new facility.

1. Determine exactly what you need for the program you operate and for the groups you serve.

2. Form a new facility task force.
3. Check to see if there are other currently used community buildings you can share.
4. Check to see if there is an existing building in the community that can be converted or renovated.
5. Check and evaluate the potential for public and private funding, before going any further.
6. If you have found an existing building, find a local expert to estimate the cost of putting the building back into working condition. Is it cheaper than constructing a new building?
7. If the construction/renovation or operating costs are too much for your group alone, can you share the building with other compatible groups?
8. Once you have found a site (for new construction or renovation), look for an architect.
9. Show at least six architectural firms over your site. Based on what they say and how you feel about them, draw up a short list of three preferred firms.
10. To your short list, ask the following questions. Mark each answer on a one to ten scale.

— What is their experience with your type of project?
— How much work have they completed over the past three years?
— How well do you think they can respond to your special requirements and your group's personalities?
— What (if any) is the firm's reputation and experience with your potential sources of funds?
— What are the firm's contacts in the community, memberships, appointments to planning boards, advisory committees, etc. — in other words, their sphere of influence?
— What is the firm's knowledge of those who might help you with the fund raising?
— How well will the architect impress people in presentation situations on your behalf?
— How does the firm combine imagination with financial reality?
— To what extent will the architect being interviewed be involved with the project (percentage of time)?
— How do they select their consulting teams, e.g., electrical, mechanical, and structural?
— Do they favour a general contractor or a project manager? How and on what basis do they select one over the other?

— Are they prepared to develop three designs for your consideration, before starting the final design?
— Can they carry out a cheap (maximum $5,000) feasibility study before going ahead with the actual design and drawings? (This study can be used to influence political bodies and sources of funds to support you. Make sure it contains an artist's rendering of how the finished building will look.)
— What is their record on cost estimates for previous assignments?
— When can they start work?
— What type of contractual arrangements will be required?

If possible, discuss your project with other groups that already have started their own construction/renovation project. It is worth traveling, to hear their experiences and advice.

Bring your architect with you when you make a major presentation. He gives you credibility.

Don't sign a contract with any firm before you have the funds in hand.

For more information about constructing or renovating a facility, contact Adelaide Court/Cour Adelaide, 57 Adelaide Street East, Toronto, Ontario.

Client dependency

*Don't do unto others as you would they should
do unto you. Their tastes may not be the same.*
George Bernard Shaw

In some urban centres, a string of social service agencies dispensing various services can be used in sequence by a client. None of the services tries to stimulate or support the client to use his own resources. None of the agencies is aware that the others are involved with the same client. The result is over-provision of services. The client's limited self-expectations are retained and he becomes totally dependent.

This is the reverse of the goal of our social services, which is the eventual self-sufficiency of each client. Co-ordination and information sharing between these agencies should be aimed at reducing client dependency and encouraging the ongoing development of personal responsibility among the people they serve.

The community storefront

People either are unaware of services not located in their neighbourhood or are intimidated by large centralized services located elsewhere. This can result in important services not reaching those who urgently need them.

As a result, many services have been decentralized and located in vacant neighbourhood stores. This not only has made these services highly available, but has nurtured a relaxed informality. The storefront may not contain all services needed in the community, but it can serve as a reassuring first contact point for referral to a centralized service.

The head office-local office relationship

I am an optimist. It does not
seem too much use being anything else.
Winston Churchill

Groups that have branches or chapters nationwide or statewide usually need a head office for co-ordination and other purposes.

Keeping a perspective on the functions and the authority of a head office is difficult once those persons who proposed and created it have left the organization. Instead of a co-ordinating tool, the head office is seen as boss!

The head office should be:
- a central point where grass-roots representatives from the local offices can decide on overall priorities for the whole organization;
- an operations unit that can provide specialized and highly practical consulting services to its branches;
- a support unit which can, on behalf of local branches or chapters, maintain relations with state or federal governments (see Chapter 11 of this manual);
- a support unit which can carry out quality and quantity monitoring of its branches or chapters.

The head office should be a tool working on behalf of its branches or chapters. Thus, control of the head office must flow from the bottom up (from the branches or chapters), not from the top down.

Grass-roots branch representatives, as head office board members, must determine the head office policies and approve its programs. The head office program and how it will affect each branch must be clearly mapped out and circulated at the beginning of each year. This will keep expectations at a reasonable level. The head office program of assistance is in response to local requests.

Each year, local branches or chapters are invited to send in written evaluations of head office services for the head office staff's and the board of directors' attention. At least once every three years, head office must sit down with each local office to determine the value of past services and what can be done in the future.

Meetings of a nation- or statewide policy-setting group, or board, usually are expensive. However, these meetings are crucial if the head office is to stay in touch with its most important constituency, the branches. To cut costs:

- Consider telephone conferences of a smaller executive group of the full policy-setting body. Keep minutes of these meetings and circulate them to the full body.
- Have local representatives from the branches or chapters assume all or part of the costs for travel and hotel expenses for head office board meetings. This decentralizes costs.
- Statewide groups can organize their branches into regional clusters (four or five, 30 to 40 miles apart). One person represents all four or five branches (as opposed to one representative each) at head office board meetings.

To maintain good head office-local branch relations don't visit local branches to fly the head office flag. Always be helpful. Following a visit, confirm in writing what you saw and heard; what you did; what you hope will happen; how you will follow up at the appropriate time; that you are available for more help if required.

It isn't good enough to give general guidelines and academic talks to local offices. Supplying how-to program kits is one way of supplying more specific and usable information. Program kits have been used by the Red Cross. For more information contact your local Red Cross chapter or write to the American National Red Cross, 17th and D Streets, Washington, D.C. 20006.

The parallel institution — a way to change things

> *I believe in getting into hot water;*
> *it keeps you clean.*
> G.K. Chesterton

One way of changing a well-established and seemingly impenetrable institution is to form a small experimental project which provides the

same service but uses different methods. The different methods may apply to systems and people who govern an organization and to those working with people using the service.

For example, free neighbourhood clinics were begun to show the need for free medical care and the need for a more intimate, neighbourhood-oriented delivery of services. Information gathered from these clinics was used systematically to persuade government and hospitals to improve their services so that they would better meet the needs of patients.

When seeking support from funding sources for the parallel institution, explain that you want to experiment with and demonstrate new ways of reaching and servicing people. Try to recruit persons from the institution or system you are hoping to change to your advisory committee. This is a positive way to send valuable information back to your target. *It is important that these persons advise, not control your project in any way.* A parallel institution (or project) can be set up with the same aims, approaches to be tested, and limited lifespan as a demonstration project.

Personal burn out

> *I didn't get sophisticated — I just*
> *got tired. But maybe that's what*
> *sophisticated is — being tired.*
> Rita Gain

People working for citizen groups do so because of an emotional as well as an intellectual commitment to an issue.

Often the group is small and without adequate resources. This results in a few people taking on the workload of many.

Beware! For short-term projects this can work. Spread over months, it almost certainly will mean that the quality of an individual's contribution will deteriorate and, in the process, he will become frustrated and possibly disillusioned, and your project could be jeopardized.

If your project doesn't collapse under the strain of over-tired volunteers or staff, the other result can be retreat to a safer, less relevant position. This is how consultants and impersonal institutions are born!

Know when to stand back and relax. Try to involve adequate numbers of people from the outset to manage the project.

Index